Steps To Prosperity

A Parable About Changing Your Financial Mindset to Build a Better Life

David G. Gatchell

Best-selling author of *The Financial Empowerment Handbook*

Four Gifts Publishing
Austin, Texas

Steps to Prosperity: A Parable About Changing Your Financial Mindset to Build a Better Life

Four Gifts Publishing, Austin, TX

This book is a work of fiction. While it contains references to financial concepts, it is intended for educational and entertainment purposes only. Any resemblance to actual events or persons, living or dead, is purely coincidental. Readers should consult a qualified financial professional before making any financial decisions.

ISBN Number 979-8-9867200-6-7 (paperback)
ISBN Number 979-8-9867200-7-4 (e-book)
Library of Congress Classification Number HG 179 DG 2025

Printed in the United States of America

Dedication

To everyone who has ever felt behind -
who's faced the weight of debt, the fog of uncertainty, or the sting of financial shame - this book is for you.

For those who were never taught, never shown, or never believed they could build a better life -
may this story be a guide, a mirror, and a spark.

> "Doing well with money has little to do with how smart you are and a lot to do with how you behave."
> - *Morgan Housel*, author of *The Psychology of Money*

You are not broken.
The system is.
And you can break free.

> "You do not rise to the level of your goals. You fall to the level of your systems."
> - *James Clear*, author of *Atomic Habits*

So let this be the moment you stop drifting.
Grow your own financial roots.
And start building the life you actually want.

TABLE OF CONTENTS

Preface

This book is a story, a financial parable about ordinary people facing the kinds of challenges that nearly all of us encounter at some point in our lives. The lessons are woven into the conversations, conflicts, and breakthroughs of a small group who gather for a community workshop on personal finance. At the center of the story is Maya, a young professional trying to find her footing. On the surface she seems to be doing fine, but underneath she is weighed down by student loans, credit card balances, and the stress of living paycheck to paycheck. She knows she should be saving and planning ahead, but the gap between knowing and doing feels wide. Bills pile up faster than progress, and financial freedom feels just out of reach.

Maya is not alone. She and her co-worker Dante, who has his own financial struggles, agree to attend a local personal finance workshop to learn how to improve their situations. At the workshop they meet Jim, a seasoned facilitator with a calm presence and a gift for making complex topics simple. Maya doesn't realize how much the experience will change her life.

In that workshop she meets others walking their own financial journeys:

Ray, a hardworking middle-aged handyman stretched thin by debt and unpredictable income.

Lisa, a single mom doing her best to keep her family afloat on one paycheck.

Sofia, eager to build a better future but unsure where to start.

Kevin, a college student determined to make smart financial decisions as he steps into adult life, but unsure what the right moves are.

Darren, an Army staff sergeant, present as an observer and contributor, preparing to one day lead workshops like this for service members and veterans.

Together, this diverse group begins to face the hard questions about money. Each week, they wrestle with concepts like budgeting, credit, debt, saving, and investing. Along the way, Maya gradually changes her mindset. Instead of seeing her situation as hopeless, she learns to celebrate small wins, paying down one debt, setting aside a little savings, resisting a purchase she would have made before. These seemingly modest choices, repeated again and again, begin to create momentum toward a stronger financial future.

That is the heart of this book: lasting financial change rarely comes from one dramatic breakthrough. It comes from a series of small shifts in our mindset, new habits, and a willingness to think differently about money.

The characters in these pages are fictional, but their circumstances are very real. Many of us know what it feels like to struggle with debt, to worry about the future, or to feel unprepared when financial surprises come our way.

If Maya can take those first steps forward, and if she and her team of financial freedom fighters can learn to build a new future together, then so can you.

Chapter 1: New Beginnings

I always thought that landing a decent job in Austin right after college would mean I had finally made it. After all, wasn't a University of Texas degree my ticket to stability and success? Yet here I was, standing in the checkout line at H-E-B with a basket of groceries, silently praying my debit card wouldn't be declined. My heart pounded as the cashier rang up the total. $83.57. I swiped my card, trying to appear casual, but inside I was anything but.

"I'm sorry, it says insufficient funds," the cashier said softly, leaning in as if sharing a secret. My cheeks burned hot. I fumbled for my credit card, hands trembling. There was no way I was going to abandon a week's worth of groceries over a few dollars. The line behind me seemed to grow longer and louder with each passing second.

"Uh, try this one," I muttered, forcing a smile as I handed over my credit card. My last resort. The card that already carried a balance I tried not to think about. This time, thankfully, the payment went through. I exhaled and mumbled a quick thanks, avoiding eye contact with the people behind me, and hurried out into the warm Texas evening.

Outside the store, I heaved the grocery bags into the backseat of my aging Honda Civic. The air was thick with humidity even as the sun dipped low over the Austin skyline. I sat in the driver's seat for a moment, forehead against my hands on the steering wheel, fighting tears of frustration. How did I get here?

Just two years ago, I graduated from UT Austin with a bachelor's in communications, full of hope and optimism. I'd been the first in my family to graduate college. My mom had thrown a huge barbecue celebration in our hometown of San Antonio, bragging to everyone that her daughter was going to "change the world." I moved to Austin permanently, thinking this city of music, tech startups, and endless breakfast tacos would be the place where I built my dream life.

In some ways, I had landed on my feet. At 24, I scored an entry-level marketing job at a trendy software startup downtown. It paid better than the retail and waitressing gigs I'd done through school, but $50,000 a year in a city like Austin only stretched so far, especially with high student loans hanging over my head. I graduated with a total of $23,500 in debt, but with interest calculated over a 10 year payment plan the total grew to $30,000 which meant I had to pay $250 every month. I rented a two-bedroom apartment off Riverside with my friend Kayla, and between rent, utilities, loan payments, and basic living expenses, my paychecks evaporated faster than summer rain on hot pavement.

Two years later, now 26, the shine had worn off. Austin's booming economy meant rising rents and pricier everything. I loved my job and this vibrant city, but each month seemed to bring a new financial strain. An unexpected car repair, an out-of-pocket dental bill, helping Mom with a bit of cash when she came up short, there was always something.

In an effort to make ends meet, I'd even started driving for Uber on weekends to earn some extra cash. My regular marketing job was a W-2 position with a steady paycheck and taxes already withheld, but the Uber gig paid me as an independent contractor, a 1099 job, so whatever I made came with no deductions and a tax headache waiting at year-end. It felt like all my "free" time went into ferrying passengers around Austin's busy streets: Saturday nights shuttling tourists and college kids from the bars on Sixth Street, Sunday mornings driving bleary-eyed travelers to the airport. The extra income helped a bit, but between paying for gas, the wear and tear on my aging Civic, and starting each week exhausted, it barely felt worth it. Even with those hours behind the wheel, I was still just scraping by.

I had maxed out one credit card and was chipping away at another. Payday was a week away, and tonight's grocery embarrassment proved what I'd been dreading: I was flat-out broke.

I took a deep breath, started the car, and pulled out of the parking lot. Driving home, I wound through the familiar streets of South Austin. Neon signs for food trucks and bars flickered on as dusk settled. Normally, I'd find this twilight hour comforting, the city coming alive with music spilling from open doors on South Congress and the aroma of grilled meat in the air. But tonight, I barely noticed. My mind was replaying the scene at H-E-B on a loop, each time sinking me deeper into shame.

As I turned onto our street, I saw a group of students in burnt-orange UT shirts jogging by, likely freshmen on an evening run. It reminded me of simpler times on campus, when my worries were mostly about exams and finding parking, not about making rent. I envied them, the hope and excitement they carried, oblivious to what awaited after graduation.

In our apartment, Kayla had taken up residence on the couch, laptop on lap and staring intently at her wide screen plugged in on the coffee table. She had taken a different path than I did, working different retail and restaurant jobs after high school before enrolling in Austin Community College's

Software Developer Bootcamp. We met while both of us were looking for housing after graduation.

Her 6-month bootcamp put her in $10,000 of student debt, but she diligently paid this off over the next two years by living frugally and working a full time day job and also freelancing in the evenings. She continued working hard, day and night but always seemed to just be scraping by. We often commiserated over being broke, but at least she handled it well. I had a full-time job and still felt one small crisis away from disaster.

"Hey Maya," she greeted me, looking away from her screens. She eyed the grocery bags in my arms. "Oh good, you went to the store. I'm making spaghetti later, if you want in."

"Sure," I mustered a smile. Spaghetti again. Cheap and filling, our go-to meal the last week before payday.

As I unpacked the groceries, I felt Kayla's eyes on me. "You okay? You look stressed."

I hesitated. No point hiding it; she knew me too well. "My card declined at H-E-B. Had to use the credit card... again."

"Ouch," she winced sympathetically. "I'm sorry. That sucks." She hopped off the couch and came over, lowering her voice as if conspiring. "If you need to borrow like twenty bucks until payday, I'm good for it. I just got paid for my last project."

I shook my head. "Thanks, but I'll manage. I hate that I'm 26 and still scrounging like a college kid. It's humiliating."

Kayla gave me a side hug. "It's tough out there. Half my workmates are drowning in student loans or credit card debt too. They just don't talk about it. It's crazy, software developers make good money yet most of us struggle with groceries towards the end of the month and have zero savings!" She started boiling water for pasta as I put away the last can of store-brand tomato sauce.

"I just..." my voice faltered as I leaned against the kitchen counter. "I feel like I'm failing at being an adult. I went to college, got the job, did everything I was supposed to, why am I living paycheck to paycheck?" My eyes stung with frustrated tears that I tried to blink away.

Kayla stirred the pasta and looked at me thoughtfully. "Honestly? They don't teach us this stuff. We spent four years in high school learning about history, calculus, chemistry, whatever, but not a single class on how to actually manage money in the real world. Its frustrating." She shrugged. "I'm learning as I go too. Overdrafted last month, cried for an hour about it. It happens."

I sighed. "I just keep thinking, what would Mom say if she knew? She was so proud at my graduation... I feel like I'm letting her down now."

"You're being way too hard on yourself. Austin's expensive, life is expensive. And your mom would be proud of you no matter what."

I nodded, not entirely convinced. My mom, who raised me by herself while working two jobs, had instilled a fierce work ethic in me. She also drilled into me the importance of getting an education to escape the cycle of hardship she lived in. I had done that, but now I felt like I was sliding backwards.

We ate our simple dinner in the living room on the thrift-store table, chatting about Kayla's side gig and the drama with her latest app build out.. I tried to focus, but my mind wandered. The embarrassment at the store lingered like a bad taste.

After cleaning up, I retreated to my room with my laptop. Maybe I could find some quick tips online, like those articles that pop up now and then, "10 ways to save money fast" or "How to get out of debt." I had read a few, but never really followed through. Still, I typed "budgeting tips young adult" into the search bar and began scrolling through results.

The advice was mostly things I already knew: make a budget, cut unnecessary expenses, start an emergency fund, blah blah. It all sounded simple in theory, but in practice I always ended up derailed by something. And the examples seemed written by people who assumed everyone had parents to fall back on or extra cash lying around. One article cheerily suggested saving $500 a month by skipping takeout and lattes. I snorted, if I had an extra $500 each month, I wouldn't be in this mess.

Frustrated, I closed the laptop. As I did, an ad on the sidebar caught my eye. It was bright orange (maybe that's why it registered, UT colors) and read:

Free Personal Finance Workshop –
Take Control of Your Money!

Struggling with debt? Living paycheck to paycheck? Join our free 5-part community workshop and learn how to build wealth on any income.
Starts Tuesday 7pm at Carver Library, East Austin.
Hosted by Prospera Literacy (Nonprofit)
All ages welcome. Snacks provided.

I stared at the ad. It almost felt like a sign, a bit too on-the-nose for my liking. Tuesday at 7pm... that was tomorrow. I checked the date and time on my laptop. Yes, tomorrow evening. I didn't have plans, other than maybe sulking at home. East Austin wasn't far, and free snacks were appealing given my tight budget for food.

Would it be worth going? A free finance workshop might just be someone trying to sell insurance or a scammy program. But what did I have to lose? If nothing else, free snacks.

I had to admit, I was desperate for any help at this point. Maybe if I could pick up even a few real tips on managing money, I wouldn't need to spend every weekend driving for Uber just to stay afloat. The idea of not having to rely on that side hustle, and maybe even getting my weekends back, felt like a distant dream, but it was exactly what I longed for.

I shut the laptop and flopped onto my bed, feeling equal parts skeptical and hopeful. What if this workshop could actually help me figure things out? I tried not to get my hopes up, but a tiny spark of optimism flared. At the very least, maybe I'd meet others in the same boat and not feel so alone in my worries.

Clutching that thought, I set an alarm on my phone for 6pm tomorrow – enough time to get home from work and drive to the library. As I did, I realized the tightness in my chest had eased just a little. I had a plan, a next step.

Maybe, just maybe, tomorrow night could be the start of something new. With that in mind, I closed my eyes and drifted off, the sounds of distant music and city life lulling me to sleep, and the faint hope of a better future on the horizon.

Chapter 2: Setting the Foundation

Work dragged on the next day, my mind only half on the tasks at hand. As I tweaked social media copy for our startup's latest app update, the numbers swirling in my personal life kept intruding. How was I going to stretch $27 (the exact amount I'd found in my checking account that morning) over the next six days?

I felt a knot in my stomach. If any surprise expense came up, or worse, if I lost my job, I'd be in serious trouble. Our startup wasn't exactly stable; one bad month and I could be out of work with no safety net. The idea of my paycheck disappearing made my pulse quicken. I had no cushion, nothing to catch me if I fell.

At lunchtime, I pushed aside thoughts of money long enough to join my coworker Dante for a quick bite from a food truck near our office. The aroma of fried plantains and spices wafting from the Venezuelan truck was irresistible, and Dante insisted on treating me to an arepa when he noticed I was hesitating to spend.

"My treat, don't worry about it," he had said, handing the vendor a $20 before I could protest.

As we sat on a bench under the shade of a live oak, I gave him a grateful smile. "I'll pay you back next week."

"Nah," Dante waved it off. "Consider it payment for being my sounding board during all those boring client calls." He grinned, but I could tell he knew something was up with me.

We'd started at the company around the same time and bonded over being UT alumni (though we hadn't known each other in school). Dante was easygoing and quick with a joke, but I also knew he was ambitious, constantly talking about tech projects he wanted to launch, or the MBA he might go back for. If anyone else at work understood financial stress, it was probably him; he'd once mentioned having student loans and a car payment that ate up a chunk of his salary.

I unwrapped the foil from my arepa slowly. "Thanks. I... I had kind of a rough night. Money stuff."

He took a bite and nodded knowingly. "Join the club. I had to push back my car loan payment this month. They gave me a one-week grace period. It's getting tight."

It was oddly comforting to hear him admit that. We didn't usually talk about personal finances, who does?, but I felt a surge of relief at not having to pretend.

"I actually saw this ad online for a free financial literacy seminar," I ventured. "It's tonight at the Carver Library. I'm thinking of going, see if I can learn something to get my act together. Maybe it will be less depressing than googling stuff alone at midnight."

Dante raised his eyebrows. "At the library? I think I saw a flyer about that in the break room. A personal finance workshop or something, right? Some nonprofit thing."

I nodded, surprised. "Yeah, that's the one. You considered going?"

He shrugged. "I did, actually. I mean, I could use some tips. I make decent money now but somehow I've got nothing to show for it. Might be good to figure out how to not be broke by next payday, you know?" He gave a half-chuckle.

"Exactly," I sighed, then gave him a more hopeful look. "So, you want to come with? Strength in numbers?"

"Sure, why not. Free snacks, right?" he winked.

I asked Kayla to join when our paths crossed after work, and though she was super excited about it, the timing didn't work for her with her current evening freelance workload. "I'll let you know if I can make a future session. I know I need to learn this stuff," she muttered.

That evening, I navigated through East Austin to the library, an old brick building nestled between a community garden and a playground. The sun was just setting, casting a warm glow on the mosaic mural that adorned the library's wall. It depicted children reading beneath a giant pecan tree, a scene of growth and hope. Fitting, I thought, as I climbed the steps.

Inside, a librarian directed us to a meeting room. Dante and I walked in to find a circle of chairs had been arranged. A few people milled about, and against the far wall was indeed a table with snacks: a couple boxes of cookies, a veggie platter, and a jug of iced tea. On the whiteboard up front was written:

Personal Finance Workshop

Session 1 – Your Financial Foundation

A tall man with brownish hair and a neatly trimmed salt-and-pepper beard approached us with a friendly smile. He looked to be in his late fifties, wearing jeans and a polo shirt with the UT Longhorn logo. "Welcome! Here for the workshop? Sign-in sheet's right over there. I'm Jim, by the way." He shook our hands warmly.

"Hi, I'm Maya, and this is Dante," I said. We scribbled our names on the sheet which had the heading "Personal Finance Workshop." Only about eight names were listed so far.

"Glad you two could join us, Maya and Dante. Please help yourselves to snacks and have a seat anywhere. We'll get started in just a couple minutes," Jim said.

As he turned to greet others, I exhaled. I wasn't sure what I'd expected, maybe someone more intimidating or preachy. But Jim's laid-back, kind demeanor put me at ease.

Dante nudged me. "This looks legit. And hey, cookies!" He grabbed a couple of oatmeal cookies, and I poured iced tea into small paper cups for both of us.

We took seats in the circle. A moment later, an older woman in a floral blouse seated herself next to me. "Hello," she offered shyly. I noticed she had kind eyes but looked a bit tired, perhaps mid-thirties though her streaks of gray hair suggested she had seen her share of stress. "I'm Lisa," she introduced, and I caught a faint trace of a Spanish accent.

"I'm Maya. Nice to meet you," I replied, smiling.

Around the circle, a couple of others settled in: a young guy who couldn't have been older than twenty, wearing a UT baseball cap and nervously bouncing his leg; a woman about my age with a clipboard and pen ready, who looked like she came straight from the office still in a blouse and slacks; and a man who appeared in his 40s, with paint-stained pants, perhaps a construction or handyman type, who offered a polite nod when I glanced his way.

Jim took a seat and clapped his hands lightly. "Alright everyone, it's just past 7. Why don't we get started? First off, welcome. This is the first session of our five-part personal finance workshop. I'm really glad you all made it here and are investing in yourselves tonight."

He had an air about him that commanded attention, not in an authoritarian way but in confidence and warmth. I found myself sitting up a little straighter. "I look forward to working with you all every week for the first month and then a month later for our final session. This format allows you to learn and try the tips and tricks we discuss and then come back afterwards and share your experiences with the entire group. We've found this structure has worked well in other setting so I'm confident you're going get value out of our time together."

"So, I know everyone is here because you want to change something about your financial situation," Jim continued. "Maybe you're feeling overwhelmed by debt, maybe you never learned how to manage money, or you're just looking for tips to build a better future for your family. Whatever it is, this is a safe space to talk about money, a topic we usually consider pretty taboo, right?" He chuckled. A few people smiled or nodded.

"Let's start with some quick introductions. Just your first name, what made you come tonight, and one financial goal or concern you have. I'll go first to break the ice." He cleared his throat. "I'm Jim. I'm a volunteer with Prospera Literacy, and I've lived in Austin for 30 years. I used to work in finance, was a financial advisor for a long time. I'm here because I love helping people get a handle on their money; I truly believe financial literacy can change lives. A financial goal for me these days... well, I'm nearing retirement, so I'm making sure I've got enough saved to travel with my wife and maybe someday spoil some grandkids." He winked.

We laughed lightly, and I felt the tension ease.

The woman with the clipboard went next. "Hi, I'm Sofia. I'm 29. I teach English at Travis High School." She pushed a strand of dark brown hair behind her ear. "I'm here because even though I have a steady job, I feel like I'm constantly juggling bills. I want to learn how to save up, maybe buy a house one day. Right now that feels impossible on a teacher's salary. So... yeah, I'm hoping to get some tips and not feel so anxious about money all the time."

I appreciated her openness. Buying a house, yes, that felt impossible to me too, but part of me also harbored that dream.

Next was the young guy in the UT cap. He spoke in a rush. "I'm Kevin, I'm 21, a senior at UT. I uh, mostly came because I realized I have no idea how to manage money and I don't want to mess up when I graduate. Also, I blew through my summer internship money way too fast. So... figure it's better to learn now than later."

Jim nodded. "Smart thinking, Kevin. Senior year is a great time to start planning ahead."

For a moment, the room was quiet, until the broad-shouldered man with the military haircut cleared his throat. He sat up even straighter and spoke in a steady tone:

"Darren Jacobs. I serve with the U.S. Army, Military Intelligence Battalion, 1st Cavalry Division, Fort Hood. I've also recently stepped into a volunteer role helping to lead financial literacy programs. I'm here in Jim's class today to experience it the same way participants do, so I can learn how it's conducted before I help guide future groups. My hope is to take what I learn and share it with others, especially fellow service members and veterans, so they can avoid the financial struggles I've seen too often." He gave a single polite nod and fell silent.

Jim nodded respectfully. "Thank you, Darren, and thank you for your service. Darren's here tonight not just to learn, but to observe how the class runs and to contribute his perspective where it fits. He'll be helping guide groups like this in the future, so we're glad he's experiencing it firsthand alongside us."

Darren merely shifted in his seat, saying nothing more. We took his cue and continued around the circle.

The man in paint-spattered clothes spoke with a slight drawl. "Name's Ray. I'm 45. I do drywall and painting for a living. Work is on and off. My kids are in middle school and I want to figure out how to get some savings for their college or at least not live job to job. One day I'd like to work for myself, make more money and be more in control. Also wouldn't mind being able to fix up my truck without maxing out my Visa." He gave a small grin that made everyone chuckle; we could all relate to that.

Then it was my turn. I swallowed, feeling my face heat up. "I'm Maya, 26. I work in marketing. And... well, I came because I feel like I'm making okay money but I don't know where it all goes. I have student loans and credit card debt that's stressing me out. I guess my goal is to just not feel panicked when an unexpected expense comes up, and maybe actually start saving for something beyond next month."

Beside me, Dante gave me an encouraging nod.

He then introduced himself. "I'm Dante, 27. I work with Maya. I'm here because even though I make more than I ever have in my life, I'm still living paycheck to paycheck too. I got student loans, and I admit I'm not the best at budgeting. I want to learn how to invest, actually. Like, I hear people at work talking about stocks or crypto or whatever and I'm clueless. So yeah, I want to get on track for the future."

After Dante, it was Lisa's turn, the woman next to me. She gave a hesitant smile. "Hi, I'm Lisa. I'm 34. I have a daughter, she's eight. I came because I want to learn how to provide a better life for her. I'm a dental receptionist, and it's just me and her. Lately it's been hard with prices going up on everything... sometimes I worry I'll never be able to save for her college or even emergencies. So, I guess my goal is stability for my little girl and maybe buying a home far in the future, if I can."

Her voice trembled just a bit at the end. Instinctively, I reached over and squeezed her hand lightly. She gave me a grateful look. I could feel my heart ache for her situation, doing it all alone.

Jim looked around, his gaze kind. "Thank you all for sharing. It takes a lot to just open up about money challenges. Like I said, we usually don't talk about these things openly, so I commend you all for that courage. Give yourselves a hand, seriously."

A few of us clapped softly, a gentle, supportive round.

"I want you all to know," Jim went on, "that no matter what your situation is, whether it's debt, low income, lack of knowledge, there are steps you can take to improve it. I've seen people from all walks of life, folks who thought they'd never get out of a hole, turn things around. It might be a slow process, but it is possible. And you're starting that journey tonight by being here."

I felt a little flutter of hope. Maybe this wasn't going to be a waste of time after all.

Jim stood up and grabbed a marker. "Over the next two months, we'll cover some key topics: budgeting, managing debt, saving strategies, investing basics, and planning for long-term goals like buying a home or retirement. Think of these as tools in your financial toolbox." He wrote the topics in big letters on the whiteboard as he spoke:

Key Topics

Budgeting

Debt

Saving

Investing

Future Planning

"But first, we need to start with getting a clear picture of where we each stand now. For the rest of tonight, we're going to talk about budgeting and cash flow, essentially understanding your income and expenses. It might sound basic, but you'd be surprised how many people, even high earners, don't truly know where their money goes each month."

I straightened in my chair. This was definitely me, half the time I was afraid to even total up my monthly expenses. Ignorance felt safer, until it wasn't.

Jim drew a simple chart on the pad: two columns with headers Income and Expenses.

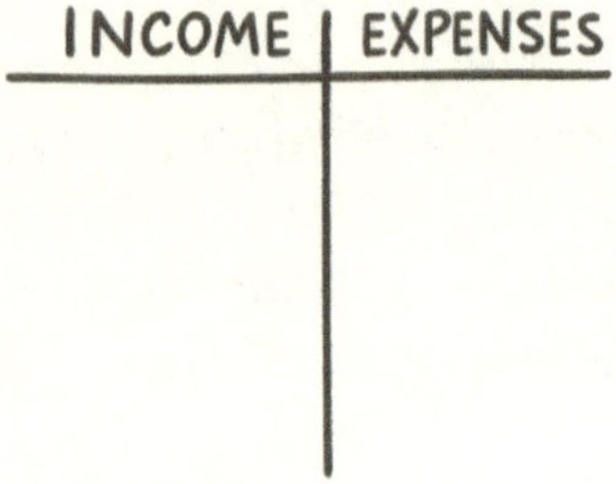

"A budget is just a plan for your money," he said. "And the first step to making a plan is knowing what's coming in and what's going out. So, for homework, yes, I'm giving you homework," he smiled as a few people groaned good-naturedly, "I want each of you to track your expenses for the next week. Write down every dollar you spend, whether it's a bill you pay, gas for your car, a coffee, anything. If you have old bank statements or a banking app that categorizes things, even better, take a look at the last month or two. The idea is to come back next week with a clearer picture of your money flow."

Kevin, the college student, raised his hand. "Do we need to bring in like our actual budgets or share our numbers?"

"No, no, nothing public unless you're comfortable," Jim assured. "This is for you. We might discuss general observations, but you won't have to disclose specifics if you don't want to. The goal is for you to have data on yourself.

Think of it like step one: diagnosing the problem. If we don't know the numbers, it's hard to prescribe a solution."

That made sense. I'd avoided really looking at my whole financial picture out of fear, but being here, buoyed by the presence of others in the same boat, I felt brave enough to try.

"Also," Jim added, "if you have debts, credit cards, loans, what have you, try to list out the balances and interest rates for yourself. We won't share those in detail either, but knowing the totals is important for tackling them later."

I swallowed. That meant I'd have to finally peek at my credit card statements I'd been shoving into a drawer. Not fun, but necessary.

The conversation turned more casual after that. Jim asked if anyone had tried budgeting before or used any apps. Sofia mentioned she used a Google Sheet to track her expenses but wasn't sure how to categorize things. Dante admitted he tried an app that yelled at him for overspending but he ended up deleting it. Lisa said she mostly just paid bills as they came and prayed her paycheck would cover everything.

Jim listened and responded with encouragement, sharing a couple of simple tips like, "Try to categorize your spending into needs versus wants," and "Don't beat yourself up over past mistakes; we're looking forward. You don't wake up one morning with perfect finances. It starts with small shifts, like writing down your spending, that feel almost too simple. But over time, those shifts compound into big results."

By the end of the session, I noticed the nervous energy I'd walked in with had transformed into something else, determination. We all lingered a bit, finishing the iced tea and chatting.

Sofia and I exchanged numbers when we realized we both lived near Riverside. "Maybe we can get coffee or, like, free coffee at work or something and compare notes on this stuff sometime," she joked, acknowledging our budgets. I liked her immediately; she was practical but had a sense of humor.

I also learned that Dante and Kevin both lived up north near campus, and that Ray had driven in from Pflugerville, a suburb to the north. Lisa had brought her daughter, who was reading in a corner of the library with headphones on during the workshop. A bright kid named Marisol; I waved to her and she shyly waved back as they left.

As we all headed out into the warm night air, I found myself walking with Dante to the parking lot. The streetlights had flickered on, casting a gentle glow on the quiet neighborhood street lined with pecan trees.

"So, that wasn't so bad," Dante said, hands in his pockets. "Kinda nice hearing everyone's stories. I half expected some boring lecture, but Jim's cool."

"Yeah," I agreed. "I actually... I feel a bit better. Like maybe this is doable if we all stick it out."

He nodded. "Accountability helps, I guess. Hey, maybe we should meet up this weekend and work on the 'homework' together? Like, go through our bank statements or something. Misery loves company." He laughed.

I considered it. Usually I guarded my money mess like a deep dark secret, but Dante had been surprisingly open tonight. "I'd like that. We could, I don't know, hit a coffee shop with Wi-Fi. Or the library again even."

"Let's do Saturday afternoon. How about Cherrywood Coffeehouse up off Manor Road? They have Wi-Fi and good iced coffee. We can bring laptops, try to make sense of our spending."

It sounded almost... fun? At least a lot less daunting than doing it alone. "Deal. Text me the details?"

He gave a thumbs up and headed toward his car. "You got it. And Maya?"

"Yeah?" I looked up from fishing my keys out of my purse.

"I'm glad you found that flyer. I think this might actually help. I feel kinda hopeful, you know?"

His tone was earnest, with a hint of surprise, as if he didn't often admit to hope. It made me smile. "Me too, Dante. Me too."

I drove home that night with the windows down, letting the balmy breeze flow through to clear my mind. The city lights of downtown twinkled in my rearview as I crossed the bridge back to South Austin. It struck me that for the first time in a long while, I felt something other than dread when thinking about money. It wasn't that I suddenly had more money or any concrete solutions yet, but I had a sense of direction, and a small community of others to lean on.

Tomorrow, I'd open up those bank statements and credit card bills. It was time to face the numbers. This time, I wouldn't do it in fear and isolation, but with the knowledge that I wasn't alone in this journey.

That weekend, Dante and I followed through on our plan. Saturday afternoon found us huddled over our laptops at a corner table in Cherrywood Coffeehouse, a spread of receipts and bank statements between us. The rich scent of coffee mingled with our sighs as we started sorting through a week's worth of expenses.

"Okay, let's see," Dante muttered, scrolling through his banking app. "Fixed expenses: rent, car payment, insurance... those are the same every month. Variable expenses: looks like I spent way too much on eating out and random Amazon buys." He shook his head. "Man, I didn't realize I blew so much on takeout. No wonder I'm always broke by payday."

I winced in recognition. "Tell me about it. I added up what I spent on coffees, snacks, and rideshares, it's embarrassing." I had a notebook where I'd been jotting down every purchase. Seeing the totals next to categories was eye-opening. "My 'eating out' category is almost as high as my grocery bill. And I found a $30 subscription I forgot to cancel. That's money straight down the drain."

We worked quietly for a while, occasionally sharing a disbelieving laugh or groan as we uncovered our spending blind spots. It was oddly comforting to do this together, less shameful, somehow, comparing notes instead of hiding our mistakes. We even started color-coding my notebook, labeling each item with "need" or "want" as Jim had suggested. The page filled with more ink in the "want" column than I'd expected.

After an hour or so, I sat back and rubbed my eyes. "This is a wake-up call, huh?"

"No kidding," Dante said. He pushed aside his empty cold brew cup. "But, you know... it feels good to actually face it. Like ripping off a Band-Aid."

I nodded. "Yeah. I always thought looking at my spending would just make me feel awful. And it does, a little," I gave a short laugh, "but I also feel more... in control? At least now I know where the money's going."

"Exactly. Now we can start figuring out how to plug the leaks," he replied, twirling a pen between his fingers. "I might need to cook at home more. And maybe sell some of those gadgets I don't use."

"And I need to put a cap on my takeout habit," I added. "Meal prepping, here I come." The idea of spending Sunday afternoon cooking was not thrilling, but if it helped my budget, it might be worth it.

Dante glanced at me, hesitation on his face as if debating whether to say something. "Maya, can I ask you something? Do you ever worry about... like, if something happened? Like losing your job or a medical emergency?"

I chewed my bottom lip. "All the time. Honestly, after rent and bills, I barely save anything. If I got laid off, I might last a month on my own. And if I got really sick…" I gestured to the papers. "I'm not even sure how I'd pay for that. I have insurance through work, but still, the deductible alone would wipe me out." Just voicing that fear made my chest tight.

He let out a low whistle. "Same here. I don't have much of a cushion either. Kinda why I'm thinking about that MBA eventually, maybe a higher salary could help, if I can handle more student loans." He gave me a wry smile. "Crazy, right? Go into debt to maybe earn more money. It's a gamble."

"Not crazy," I said, thinking of our upcoming workshop session. "I mean, investing in yourself can pay off, but it's still scary. My degree got me this job, but I'm still paying for it." I tapped my pen on my notebook where I'd written down my student loan payments.

We shared a moment of quiet understanding. Both of us were trying to build a life on shaky foundations, no savings, debts on our backs, and that lingering fear of the what-ifs. But at least now we weren't alone in figuring it out.

Before we left the café, we set some informal goals for ourselves: he would list a few gadgets to sell online, and I promised to actually cook next week and stick to a $50 food budget. Small steps, but it felt good to have a plan. We high-fived like teammates who had just drawn up a play.

"See you Wednesday at the workshop, teammate," Dante joked as we parted ways.

"You bet. Accountability, right?" I smiled.

Chapter 3: Building Your Blueprint

By the time the second workshop session rolled around, I was equal parts nervous and excited. I had dutifully tracked every penny I spent for a week, and even though the picture wasn't pretty, I felt ready to learn more. When I walked into the Carver Library meeting room that evening the white board had been updated:

Personal Finance Workshop

Session 2 – Building Your Blueprint

I was relieved to see all the familiar faces from last time, and one new face. "Kayla!! What are you doing here?" I was surprised to see my roommate at this financial literacy seminar. Even though I had talked with her about it, I certainly didn't expect her to show up with all her current projects.

"Maya, sorry to surprise you," admitted Kayla. "I wanted to follow your lead with this financial literacy stuff, but I was too embarrassed to accept my own situation and certainly didn't want to share it with anyone else! However, after seeing how excited you were after just one class, I plucked up my courage, and I'm here. Plus my freelance client extended his app launch by a week so I can squeeze in a couple hours!"

"Well that's awesome that you came! Come lets sit together." I was excited that my roommate made it and looked forward to learning even more about her financial struggles and maybe find a way to help her.

We settled into the now-familiar circle of chairs. Jim caught my eye and gave a welcoming nod. Once everyone had helped themselves to some cookies and taken a seat, he spoke up. "Welcome back, everyone. I'm glad you all made it for session two. I see we have a new face here tonight, welcome. We usually start off by checking in on how things went during the week. But first, for the benefit of our newcomer, let's do a quick introduction. Just your name and what brought you here."

"Hi, I'm Kayla," she said softly. "I'm 26 and Maya and I are roommates. I missed last week, but I'm here now because... well, because I feel I'm drowning financially." Her voice wavered and she looked down at her hands. "I, um, I had to have an emergency appendectomy last year and I didn't have health insurance at the time. It happened so fast and..." She took a shaky breath. "Long story short, I ended up with hospital bills of about $40,000. I've been trying to pay it off little by little, but it's overwhelming. I'm afraid to even check my mail because of all the collection notices. I came tonight because I need help. I never want to feel this helpless and ashamed again."

A heavy silence fell over the room. Kayla's eyes were shiny with tears she was clearly fighting back. Instinctively, I reached over and rubbed her back comfortingly. My heart ached; I remembered her emergency room visit last year, I drove her to the hospital after all! However, I didn't know *anything* about her not having insurance or the high cost of the procedure. I assumed it was all covered and Kayla never mentioned anything different. $40,000 might as well have been $4 million if you didn't have it. And the shame in her voice, I'd felt that too, in my own way. Different cause, same sinking feeling.

Jim gave Kayla a gentle nod. "Thank you for sharing that, Kayla. That took a lot of courage. Medical debt is..." he sighed, "it's one of the leading causes of financial trouble in this country. And it often feels very unfair, because it's not like you planned to get sick. I'm so sorry you've had to go through that. I want you to know you're not alone, and there are ways to get through it. We can talk more after the session about resources that might help, okay?"

Kayla managed a grateful smile as she wiped at the corner of her eyes. "Thank you."

Ray jumped in, “thanks for sharing Kayla, that took guts. And welcome to our group.” He proceeded with his introduction, similar to last session and then we went all around the circle so everyone could introduce themselves to our new member.

With introductions done, Jim stood and addressed the group. "I'm really glad you're all here. Before we dive into new material, I want to check in: how did the homework go? Did anyone have any observations or 'aha' moments tracking your expenses this week?"

Dante and I exchanged a quick look, remembering our Saturday caffeine-fueled budget autopsy. Sofia, the teacher, raised her hand with a wry smile. "I'll go. It was... enlightening. I realized I was spending almost a hundred dollars a month on subscription services I barely use. That was a shock. I canceled two of them, actually."

"Good for you," Jim nodded approvingly. "Those subscriptions can really add up. Who else?"

Kevin leaned forward. "I saw that I spend a crazy amount on food. Like, I knew I ordered a lot of pizza and stuff, but seeing it all together... whoa. I'm definitely maxing out my campus meal plan and cutting back on Door Dash."

A few people chuckled, and he grinned sheepishly. "Yeah, lesson learned."

I decided to chime in. "I noticed a lot of my spending was on convenience, buying things because I didn't plan ahead. Like coffee because I woke up too late to make it, or takeout because I was too tired to cook. It hit me that with a little planning, I could save a lot."

"Absolutely," Jim said. "Awareness is the first step. Once you see those patterns, you can start to change them. How about fixed expenses versus variable expenses? Did anyone get a sense for how much of your budget is going to things that are fixed amounts each month versus things you have more control over?"

Ray, the drywall worker, spoke up. "I did, actually. My fixed costs, rent, truck payment, insurance, those alone eat up about 70% of my income most months. It doesn't leave a lot of wiggle room. Seeing that on paper was kind of scary."

Jim nodded. "That is eye-opening, isn't it? For a lot of people, especially with lower or variable incomes, fixed expenses take up a big chunk. And if 70% (or more) is going toward must-pay bills, it gets very tough to cover everything else, let alone save. One goal we might work toward is trying to get that fixed percentage down over time, either by reducing expenses or increasing income."

He turned to the rest of us. "If your fixed costs are too high to comfortably cover with your income, that can be a sign you're stretching too far, like maybe rent is too expensive or the car payment is a bit much. Variable expenses are where you typically have more flexibility: food, utilities, shopping, etc. Those are easier to adjust when you need to tighten the belt. The key is to identify which is which."

As Jim spoke, I found myself thinking about my own breakdown. My fixed costs were around 60% of my take-home pay, mostly thanks to the relatively cheap apartment I'd lucked into. But I had never framed it that way before, fixed versus variable. It made me see why I always felt squeezed; so much of my paycheck was spoken for before the month even started.

"Alright," Jim continued, "now that we've got a clearer picture of our spending, let's talk a bit about the other side of the equation: income. Specifically, I want to chat about how different paths in life can impact your income and your finances long-term. Some of you touched on this last week, education, career choices, that kind of thing. Education or training is one way many people try to increase their earning potential, but as we know, it can come with costs or debt. Maybe we can learn from each other's experiences here. Lisa, you mentioned you went through some vocational training. Would you mind sharing a bit about that? Like what you did and how it's playing out for you financially?"

Lisa sat up a little straighter. "Sure. Um, right out of high school I couldn't afford college. Plus, I needed to start working quickly. So I enrolled in a one-year certificate program at Austin Community College to become a medical office assistant. It was affordable, especially with grants, and I finished with no debt. That's how I got the job as a receptionist at the dentist office. It pays the bills, but..." she glanced at Kayla beside her, then continued, "it's not a lot. I'm never really ahead. So now I'm looking into going back to school to become a licensed vocational nurse or maybe an dental hygienist. Those programs are like one to two years. They cost more, and I'd probably have to take on some student loans or find childcare while I study, but the pay jump is pretty significant if I can do it." She offered a nervous smile. "I want to make a better living for my daughter and me, you know?"

"That's really inspiring," Sofia said. "Going back to school while working and parenting... I respect that so much."

Lisa smiled appreciatively. "It's scary, but I keep thinking in the long run it will be worth it. I just have to figure out how to manage financially for the year or two I'll be in school. We might have to cut back, or I might do the program part-time while still working."

Jim chimed in, "There are often scholarships or employer programs for people in your field, especially in healthcare, since there's a big need. We can try to find some resources for you, Lisa. But I think your plan of investing in your skills for a higher-paying career is a solid one. It's like a short-term sacrifice for long-term gain."

He then looked over to Kevin. "Kevin, you're in college now. How have you been thinking about the balance between the cost of school and the payoff later?"

Kevin blew out a breath. "Honestly, I didn't think about it much when I started. I just kind of always assumed I'd go to college. I'm the first in my family to go, and I got some scholarships, but I still had to take out loans for the rest. I try to keep it minimal, I'm working part-time at the campus library to cover books and rent, but it's hard to juggle work and classes. I'm studying computer science, so I'm hopeful I'll get a good job when I graduate. But I'm already about twenty grand in debt. By the time I finish, maybe thirty. That freaks me out sometimes. Like, what if I don't get a high-paying job right away? How do I even start paying that back and still afford rent and everything?" He fidgeted with the brim of his cap, the weight of that thought clearly bothering him.

Jim gave him an understanding nod. "Those are valid concerns. The good news is computer science is a field with strong earning potential, generally. So the investment might very well pay off. But you're right, student loans can be a heavy burden starting out. One thing to remember is that federal student loans usually have options, like income-driven repayment plans, so your payments stay manageable if your income is low at first. And, as a few of you might know, if you work in public service or certain fields, there are loan forgiveness programs. Sofia, you're a teacher, are you aiming for Public Service Loan Forgiveness?"

Sofia nodded. "Yeah, that's the plan. I have about $15,000 in loans from undergrad. I'm in year four of teaching, and I've been on an income-based repayment plan. If I stick with it for six more years, the rest could be forgiven. Assuming the program is still around, of course." She gave a half-smile, half-grimace, PSLF has had its controversies, I recalled.

"It's a great option if it works out," Jim said. "The key, as Kevin said, is not to let the debt prevent you from moving forward. Use the programs and plans out there. And Kevin, it's smart to work during school to minimize what you borrow. Just make sure you still have time for your studies, it's a tough balance, I know."

Dante cleared his throat. "Speaking of loans for school… I've been thinking about maybe going for an MBA in a couple years. To move up in my field. But hearing all this, I'm like, do I really want to take on, I dunno, another $40,000 in loans?" He looked around as if hoping someone had an answer.

Jim gave a thoughtful hum. "That's a big question, Dante. And it's good you're thinking about it critically. This is where the concept of Return on Investment – ROI - comes in. If you spend $40,000 on an MBA, what do you expect to get in return? Maybe a higher salary, promotions, a better network. It might boost your income by say $20,000 a year, just as an example. In a case like that, the investment could pay for itself in a couple of years of higher earnings. But if it only boosts your income a little, or you end up in a job market saturated with MBAs, maybe it takes much longer to pay off. You have to weigh it. Also consider less expensive options: part-time programs, employer sponsorships, scholarships. It's not just the cost, it's the opportunity as well."

Dante nodded slowly. "That makes sense. I guess I need to research and run the numbers, not just jump in because it sounds like a good idea."

"Exactly," said Jim. "The same goes for any education or training, always consider the cost versus the expected benefit. We heard two different paths so far tonight: Lisa's vocational route with low upfront cost but a potentially lower starting pay and Kevin's college route with more upfront cost but higher potential earnings. Now, I'd love to learn about Darren's military route." He turned to the soldier.

Darren, who had been listening quietly, straightened up. "Yes, sir," he said. I noticed he often addressed Jim like a superior officer, out of habit. "I didn't have money for college either, and I wasn't sure what I wanted to do. So I enlisted at 18. The Army provided training, and a steady paycheck. I've been in for 10 years now. The pay... well, nobody joins the military to get rich. But I have a free place to live on base, allowances for food and housing when I'm off base, and good benefits. I've been able to save a little, actually."

He cleared his throat and continued, "The big thing for me is the GI Bill. When I finish my service, I have money for college waiting for me. It will cover my tuition and even give me a housing stipend while I go to school. I'm planning to use it to get a degree in engineering when I transition out in a couple years. So, my 'ROI' was trading my time and service for an education later. Plus the Army taught me skills, leadership, mechanical training, that I can use in civilian jobs."

"That's a great perspective," Jim said, and a few of us murmured agreement. I found myself admiring Darren; he had made a calculated choice and leveraged what the military offered. Of course, he also risked a lot in the process: danger, stress, years away from family. But financially, it made sense for him.

Jim looked around the group, his gaze landing on Ray and even flicking to me and Dante. "There are so many paths. Some involve debt, some don't. Some pay off quickly, others slowly. What's important is that you think about the trade-offs like we just discussed. For those of you considering further education or training, research the earning potential in that field and the cost of the programs. And remember, it's not just dollars and cents, it's also about what will make you happy or fulfilled. But since we're here to talk finances, it's smart to go into those decisions with clear eyes."

My mind was buzzing. I had never really considered how differently each person's choices could play out financially, beyond just the vague idea that more education equals more money. Hearing it laid out like this, though, I understood why Jim called this whole session a "wake-up call." We were all waking up to the reality of cause and effect in our money lives: spend without thinking and you'll be in trouble, invest in yourself and it might pay dividends, ignore risks like health insurance and you could end up like poor Kayla, overwhelmed by a random catastrophe.

The conversation shifted to more immediate concerns after that. Jim opened the floor for any pressing questions, and Kayla timidly raised her hand. "Um, what should someone in my situation do? With the medical bills?" She looked almost embarrassed to ask, but we were all rooting for her, I could feel it.

Jim answered gently, "Medical debt can be really tough. First, I'd say communicate with the hospital or providers if you haven't already. Sometimes they have financial assistance programs or can reduce the bill for low-income patients. Even setting up a zero-interest payment plan is better than letting it go to collections. There's also nonprofit credit counselors who can help negotiate on your behalf. We can talk more after and I can give you some contacts. And, moving forward, as hard as it is, getting some kind of health insurance is crucial, even if it's a high-deductible plan just to protect against the big stuff."

Kayla nodded, blinking back tears again. I gave her shoulders another squeeze of support. I realized both Lisa and I were holding Kayla's hands now, and we exchanged a small smile across her. In that moment, none of us felt like strangers.

Before wrapping up, Jim introduced one last concept. "Alright, I know we covered a lot tonight, great job, everyone, by the way. Before we go, I want to introduce the idea of net worth, since we'll touch on that more in future sessions. Has anyone here ever calculated their net worth?"

Most of us shook our heads or stared blankly. I knew the general idea but had never actually added everything up.

"Okay," Jim smiled. "Simply put, your net worth is everything you own minus everything you owe. Think of it as your financial big picture number. If you sold everything you have—your car, your savings, maybe any valuables—and paid off all your debts, what would be left? That can be a negative number or a positive number. A lot of young people, or folks who've been through something like a foreclosure or medical crisis, might have negative net worth. That's okay, for now. It's just a starting point. The goal over time is to turn it positive and keep it growing."

He erased a section on the whiteboard and sketched a simple equation:

Assets – Liabilities = Net Worth

Under Assets he listed examples: cash, savings, car value, home equity, investments. Under Liabilities: credit card debt, student loans, car loan, mortgage, medical debt.

Then he paused and wrote a new list down the margin of the board.

"Just for perspective," Jim said, "here are the *median* net worth numbers from the Federal Reserve's 2022 Survey of Consumer Finances for each decade of age range:"

Median Net Worth's

20s: ~ $7,000

30s: ~ $45,000

40s: ~ $135,000

50s: ~ $246,000

60s: ~ $338,000

He turned back to the group. "Now, let me be clear—these are averages. And really, who here thinks of themselves as 'average' or 'typical,' anyway?" he joked, getting a few smiles. "So averages aren't the goal. But they do offer a little insight into how people your age, across the country, are generally doing. What matters more is not the national numbers, but where *you* want to be, and what changes you can make to move in that direction."

Ray let out a sharp laugh. "There's no way. I'm not even close. With my debts, I'm probably negative, not anywhere near a hundred grand. Who are these people?"

Lisa shook her head in agreement. "Yeah, same here. I'm barely scraping by. I don't have any savings or assets. Seeing numbers like that just feels impossible."

Jim gave a slow nod, his tone softening. "I hear you both. And you're right, many people are negative, especially early on or after a tough setback. Remember, those numbers are medians, not minimums. Plenty of people fall below them. The point isn't to compare yourselves or feel defeated. It's to see what's possible and use it as motivation. Every bit of debt you pay down, every dollar you save, moves you forward. Over time, your number will grow, and that's what matters."

Ray frowned thoughtfully. "So what, are these people just keeping like $135,000 sitting in a savings account somewhere? Because I can't even imagine that."

Jim chuckled. "Not usually. For most folks in their 40s or 50s, the bulk of their net worth isn't cash, it's in their home. Equity they've built up as they've paid down their mortgage. They might also have retirement accounts, like a 401(k) or IRA, that add to that total. But the part sitting in savings or checking is usually much smaller. That's why it's important to look at the whole picture, not just what's in your bank account."

Darren cleared his throat. "Jim's right. Most of the younger soldiers I work with have negative net worth, student loans, car loans, credit cards, but that doesn't mean they're stuck there forever. I've seen plenty who started in the red, then, after a few years of steady pay and saving, started to climb out. It's not about where you are today, it's about building habits so that five or ten years from now, you're in a better spot. The key is just to start."

Jim nodded appreciatively. "Exactly. It's about the direction you're moving, not the snapshot today."

He let the room absorb this for a moment. "When you go home this week, try making a list of all your assets and what they're roughly worth, and all your debts and their balances. Even if it's scary or depressing, it's important. When you see that number, don't panic. Think of it as a baseline. We're going to talk about ways to improve it by increasing assets, decreasing debts, or both."

I swallowed hard. I could already guess my net worth: a few thousand in my 401(k) and some old savings bonds my grandma gave me, minus my student loans and credit card debt... I was likely deep in the red. But oddly, I felt less afraid to face it now. I'd ripped off the Band-Aid with tracking my spending; I could do it with this too. Jim was right, it was just a number, a starting point.

As we packed up to leave, the room hummed with a different energy than a week ago. Still serious, but hopeful. I overheard Ray asking Darren for advice on negotiating a used car price, and Sofia and Kevin comparing notes on cheap meal ideas for busy schedules. We were all helping each other, bit by bit.

I found myself next to Kayla as we threw away paper cups and napkins from the snack table. "I'm really glad you came tonight," I told her. "That took a lot of bravery to share."

She looked at me with tired eyes but smiled. "Thanks. I almost didn't come. I wanted to tell you after my hospital stay but I still thought I could fight the charges, it was an emergency after all, right? I quickly learned that little ole me going up against the massive hospital system, I didn't stand a chance. As reality sunk in I was so ashamed about the debt... I didn't tell *anyone.* Everyone here has been so kind though, and it helps to know I'm not the only one struggling."

"Definitely not the only one," I said, shaking my head. "We're all just trying to figure it out. But we're doing it together now."

"If I can't make it to the other sessions will you promise to share your notes with me?" she asked, with sincerity in her still shaky voice. "I really need to get better with my finances, but you know my usual evening work schedule."

"Yes of course, and you can also use me as a trusted resource anytime!" I said while giving her a side hug.

As we walked to my car I felt a sense of resolve washing over me. Yes, the reality of our financial situations could be harsh, Kayla's story was proof of that. But we were learning and taking action. We weren't powerless. On the drive home, I caught myself making a mental checklist of things to do: cancel another unnecessary subscription I'd spotted, check my work sponsored health insurance to see exactly what's covered so I can fully understand this benefit and not be surprised later, and maybe even hunt for a higher-interest savings account for the tiny emergency fund I was starting to build. These were small moves, but they made me feel like I was finally steering the ship of my life rather than just drifting.

That night, I updated my spreadsheet with all my account balances and debts, bracing myself for the net worth calculation.

Net Worth = Assets - Liabilities			
Assets		**Liabilities**	
401(k)	$3,000	Credit Cards	$7,200
Investments	$1,000	Student Debt	$24,000
Savings	$0		
Total	$4,000	Total	$31,200
Net Worth =	**-$27,200**		

It was roughly negative $27,000, yikes. Seeing that number stung, a stark reminder of my student loans and credit card mistakes. But instead of despair, I pinned that piece of paper on my bulletin board, determined. It felt like drawing a line in the sand. *This is where I stand now,* I thought, *but it's not where I'll be forever.*

Falling asleep, I reflected on how much had changed in just a week. What started as a desperate trip to a workshop was turning into something else entirely. A wake-up call, yes, but also the beginning of a plan, a path forward. And I was walking that path with others now, which made all the difference in the world.

Chapter 4: Budget Breakthroughs

Saturday afternoon found me hunched over my laptop at a corner table of Cherrywood, receipts and bank statements spread out like a tactical battle plan. The aroma of espresso mingled with the chatter of other patrons, but I was laser-focused on one thing: figuring out where all my money had gone last month.

True to his word, Dante showed up, laptop in tow. To my pleasant surprise, Sofia joined us as well. I had texted her an invite that morning, figuring the more the merrier (or at least, the less awkward diving into finances would be). She had eagerly accepted, saying she could use the moral support.

"Alright, ready to face the music?" Dante asked as he pulled up a chair. He had already gotten himself an iced coffee and one for me, which I gratefully accepted. Sofia arrived moments later with a tea in hand, and we turned our table into an impromptu budgeting war room.

It turned out to be oddly comforting, even humorous at times. We compared notes and gasped or groaned at each other's spending revelations.

"I spent $250 on eating out... *in one month*!" I exclaimed, eyes wide as I totaled up charges from tacos, coffee runs, and happy hour snacks. Seeing it all together was sobering. "That's like my whole grocery budget... no wonder I'm always short."

Sofia gave a weak laugh. "Try being a teacher during football season. I spent nearly $100 on classroom decor and supplies that my school wouldn't reimburse. And I thought my biggest expense was going out with friends on weekends." She pointed at her spreadsheet. "Groceries: $300, Dining out:

$120, Classroom stuff: $95, random Target runs: oh man... $180. How did I even..." She shook her head.

Dante raised his hand as if in class. "Confession: I apparently have a $60-a-month comic book habit. I did not realize it was that much. Plus, I seriously need to stop Ubering everywhere. That's another $150." He frowned at his screen, though he still had a hint of a smile. "Hey, at least I'm supporting the local comic store economy, right?"

We all chuckled. It felt good to laugh at our own missteps, less shameful, somehow, when shared among friends.

As we worked, we traded little tips. I showed them the budgeting app I decided to try, which linked to my bank and categorized expenses automatically. Sofia talked about her Google Sheet and how she color-coded categories. Dante admitted he liked the idea of the old-school envelope method, physically dividing cash for certain things, though none of us carried much cash these days.

"Maybe digital envelopes? Like separate checking accounts or something?" he mused.

"Actually, I think some banking apps let you create sub-accounts or 'buckets'," I said. "I might look into that for my savings so I don't accidentally spend what I set aside."

We ended up spending a couple of hours, and by the end each of us had a rough budget drafted for the next month. It wasn't perfect, but it was a start. I planned out my upcoming month's expenses: rent $800, utilities $100, car payment $0 (thankfully my old Honda was paid off, though maintenance was another story), groceries $200, gas $80, student loan $250, minimum on credit card $100 (for now), and I allocated $50 for "fun" –

which sounded pitiful, but I knew I had to cut back somewhere. That budget would still leave me barely breaking even, but I identified some areas to trim: fewer takeouts, pausing my $40/month gym membership I rarely used, and cancelling a couple of streaming services (did I really need Netflix *and* Hulu right now?).

It was both depressing and empowering to see it all laid out. Depressing because I realized how tight things truly were; empowering because I finally felt in control, like taking the first steps to tame a wild horse.

Before we parted ways, we made a group pact to stick to our draft budgets for the month. "We got this," Dante said, holding up a fist. I bumped it, and Sofia piled her fist on top with a grin. It felt cheesy and earnest and exactly what I needed.

On Tuesday evening, we reconvened at the library for the third workshop session. This time, walking in, I felt a sense of camaraderie looking at those familiar faces. We were in this together.

Personal Finance Workshop

Session 3 -Budget Breakthroughs

Jim kicked off by asking how the expense tracking went. A few of us volunteered our experiences. Kevin, the college student, sheepishly admitted he spent more on beer and fast food than anything else. Ray said he was shocked to see how much little convenience store stops for snacks and sodas added up. Lisa quietly shared that she found a mistake in her bank statement , an auto-payment for a subscription she thought she canceled, which she'd now taken care of.

I spoke up about discovering my dining-out expenses. "I had no idea I was spending hundreds on restaurant food. I love supporting local taco joints, but I've got to cut back for now."

Jim nodded. "That's great insight. Remember, it's not about depriving yourself of everything. It's about being conscious and intentional. You can still enjoy a taco, just budget for it, and perhaps find savings elsewhere or treat it as an occasional reward rather than a daily habit."

He then segued into the night's main topic: creating a budget. He explained different methods, mentioning zero-based budgeting (assigning every dollar a job), apps like Mint and YNAB (You Need A Budget) that help track spending automatically, and the 50-30-20 rule (writing it on the board).

50-30-20 Rule

50% - Needs: rent, food, gas

30% - Wants: entertainment, subscriptions, travel

20% - Saving: emergency fund, planned, targeted

BUT - SAVING FIRST

"The 50-30-20 rule only really works if you shave off the 20% for savings from your net income FIRST every month. Don't wait until the end of the month, after spending for needs and wants, to see what's left over for saving. There won't be any!"

"So, we all know by now that the amount we earn is NOT the same as the amount we bring home, right?" Everyone nodded. "To get started with any budget," Jim said, "we need to start by talking about taxes. Anyone here know what April 15 is?"

A few groans and chuckles went around the room.

"Tax Day," said Maya.

"Right. It's when your annual income taxes are due to the IRS. Now here's something people get wrong all the time , your salary isn't what you actually take home. You've got to subtract income taxes first, and possibly payroll taxes like Social Security and Medicare."

He turned to the board and drew two bold headings:

Gross Pay **Net Pay**

"Gross pay is your total salary before anything is taken out. It comes from the Old French word *gros*, meaning whole or large, not disgusting," he added with a grin, prompting a laugh.

"Net pay is what actually lands in your bank account after taxes, insurance, and maybe retirement contributions are deducted."

He picked up a marker. "Let's say someone earns $52,000 a year. That's $1,000 per week, or about $4,333 per month gross. But after federal taxes, Social Security, Medicare, and maybe a little for health insurance, they're probably taking home around $3,600 net per month."

"What about state income tax?" Kevin asked.

"Good question. Texas has no state income tax, which is great for Texans. But if you live in a state like California or New York, they *do* have state income tax, so your take-home pay would be even less. Also, don't think that the great state of Texas operates for free. No way. What the state lacks in income tax revenues they make up for in higher-than-average property tax. Every state takes their piece!"

"And everyone has to pay payroll taxes on their earnings which cover mandatory Social Security contributions and Medicare. Social Security, as you all know, is the federal government's retirement payment for all those who work a minimum of 40 quarters (10 years). Medicare is the government's health insurance program for retirees. Combined, these two programs will take about 7.6% of your earnings.

"Also know that federal income taxes are significant, typically starting at 12% for those earning under $50,000, then jumping to 22% for those with taxable income between $50,000 and $100,000, and they progressively increase up to 37% for the highest earners."

"What's that 1040EZ form?" Sophia asked.

Jim nodded. "That's the simplified federal tax return form, great for people with very basic income situations. But most folks use the regular 1040 with a standard deduction, which for a single filer in 2025 is $15,000. That means if you made

$52,000, the first $15,000 isn't even taxed. You only pay taxes on the rest. Still, it adds up."

He then flipped to a fresh page and drew a revised sample monthly budget based on roughly $3,600 net monthly income:

Budget

- Housing (rent): $1,200
- Utilities: $200
- Transportation: $400 (car payment, gas, insurance)
- Groceries: $300
- Dining/Entertainment: $200
- Insurance/Medical: $370
- Debt Payments: $250
- Savings: $470
- Miscellaneous: $210

Debt payment + savings = 20%

"This shows a strong financial plan," Jim said. "About twenty percent of that net income is going to savings and debt repayment, which is exactly what we want. Even if you can't start at 20%, work your way up. Savings should be automatic, like a bill you pay *yourself* before you pay anyone else."

"This is just an example," he continued. "Everyone's numbers will look different. The key is making sure your needs are covered, you're allocating something to pay down debt and to savings, and you're living within your means."

"What if your expenses are more than your income?" Lisa asked, worry evident in her voice.

Jim gave a sympathetic smile. "That is unfortunately a common situation. If that's the case, you either need to find ways to cut expenses or increase income, ideally both. There's no magic solution. But even small changes can help. We can brainstorm some ideas individually if you want. And if it's a dire situation, there may be community resources or assistance for things like food or utilities that can help in the short term while you work on long-term changes."

He added, "Also remember the concept of *opportunity cost.* Opportunity cost is basically the trade-off in any spending decision, buying one thing means you won't have that money to spend on something else. For example, if you splurge on a $100 concert ticket, that's $100 you can't put toward groceries or paying a bill. Thinking about that trade-off can make it easier to cut out expenses that aren't as important."

Lisa nodded, though her brow remained furrowed. I made a mental note to check in with her later to see if she was okay.

Jim continued, emphasizing the importance of an emergency fund. "Unexpected expenses will happen. Car breaks down, medical bill, sudden job loss, that's life. If you don't have some savings to cushion those blows, you'll end up turning to credit and going further into debt. And many people are in that boat; a Federal Reserve study found that 37% of Americans don't have enough savings to cover a $400 emergency expense. My advice is to make building a small emergency fund one of your first priorities. Even $500 or $1000 can be a lifesaver. Treat it like a bill to yourself each month, even if it's just $20 at a time."

He looked around the room, making eye contact with each of us. "Remember: pay *yourself* first. This means when you get your paycheck, you set aside money for savings or investments as if it were as non-negotiable as your rent. If you wait to save what's left over, often nothing will be left over. So even if it's a small amount, put something away first. You deserve to invest in your own future security."

Suddenly, Darren cleared his throat, speaking up for the first time since his curt introduction at the first meeting. "I've actually been doing something like that," he said quietly, surprising us. It was the first time he'd volunteered to speak. "I'm in the military, and our housing is covered. I've always lived pretty modestly otherwise, so I started saving a portion of my pay from day one. About twenty percent of every paycheck, actually, straight into savings."

I saw a couple of jaws drop around the circle. Kevin blinked. "Twenty percent of your income? Since you started working?" he asked, clearly impressed.

Darren nodded as if it were no big deal. "Yes, sir. Since my first paycheck at 18. You get used to living on what's left. After a while, you don't miss the money you're saving."

Jim beamed at him. "That's outstanding, Darren. A great example of paying yourself first and living within your means. Not many people do that, over one in five Americans don't save any of their income, so you're really ahead of the game."

The rest of us murmured our amazement. I noticed Ray give a low whistle. Twenty percent of his income, saved consistently for years , the thought boggled my mind.

That phrase Jim used stuck with me: *You deserve to invest in your own future.* I'd never thought about savings like that , like paying *future me*, rather than depriving *present me.* And hearing that Darren had actually saved twenty percent of every paycheck, even on a military salary, hammered it home. Maybe saving, even a sizable chunk, was more doable than I'd assumed if I made it a priority.

As the session wrapped up, we discussed strategies to stick to our budgets. Sofia suggested meal-prepping together sometime to avoid restaurant temptation. (We all heartily agreed anything beats sad microwave dinners alone.) Kevin said he'd uninstall his food delivery apps to curb late-night spending. Dante was considering selling some old electronics and comic collectibles online to give himself a buffer for this month.

I found myself volunteering an idea too. "Kayla and I talked about doing a weekly movie night at home instead of going out. We can take turns picking a movie and cooking something cheap. That way we still hang out but save money. If anyone wants to join, you're welcome. We could even make it a potluck thing."

"Oh, by the way. Kayla misses you guys since she can't make these evening sessions due to her night job, so would love to have you all over."

Ray chuckled. "I make a mean chili. Count me in if you do that. Cheaper than taking the kids out to eat, that's for sure."

I smiled, feeling warm at the thought of our new frugal friend circle. "Chili and movie night , sounds like a plan."

After class, as we filtered out, I caught up with Lisa while her daughter, Marisol, skipped ahead down the hall. "How are you doing?" I asked gently.

She gave a small shrug. "It's a lot to take in. I did the numbers... if I'm honest, I'm barely breaking even most months. Daycare costs for after school, rent, car, everything..." She trailed off, then forced a smile. "But I'll try some of the things Jim suggested. Maybe I can pick up a few extra hours at work or do something on the side."

Impulsively, I said, "If you ever need help or just want to talk it through, you have my number. Maybe we can go over it together and see if there's anything to adjust. And that potluck movie night, I meant it. You and Marisol should come. We'll pick family-friendly movies when she's there."

Her shoulders relaxed a bit and she nodded. "Thank you, Maya. That means a lot. I'll see if I can swing it with our schedule."

Driving home that night, I reflected on how much had changed in just a week. The embarrassment of the declined card at H-E-B still stung, but now it was fueling me rather than paralyzing me. I had confronted the full picture of my finances, grim as it was, and made a plan. I had allies in this journey; people I might soon call friends. And I had small victories: saying no to an invite earlier that week to an expensive dinner (I countered with a suggestion for a cheaper taco truck meetup instead, which my friends enjoyed just as much), cooking all my meals over the weekend, and setting up an automatic transfer of $50 from each paycheck into a savings account to start building that emergency fund.

When I got home, I found Kayla at the kitchen table with her laptop and extra screen. She looked up and asked, "How was the workshop?"

"Really good, actually," I said, hanging my keys. "We missed you." I told her about some of the tips I'd learned and how I'd made a budget.

She whistled in admiration when I showed her my spreadsheet. "Dang girl, look at you. We should do a budget too for the apartment stuff. And seriously, let's do that movie night idea you mentioned. I'm down to cook at home more if it means we save money. I could use less stress about rent."

I felt grateful that Kayla was so supportive. "Thanks. Yeah, let's start this weekend. Also, I realized something: we've been buying a lot of name-brand cleaning products and stuff. Maybe we could switch to generic or cheaper options. And the AC... maybe we can keep it a tad warmer during the day to save on electricity?" (Austin's summer heat was brutal, but our last utility bill had been painful.)

"I'm game if you are. We'll get some fans going," she agreed.

It was like once I opened the door to talking about money, all sorts of ideas came freely. I no longer felt the need to pretend everything was fine. Instead, I was taking action, however small.

That night, as I updated my budget with the week's expenses (a few dollars for coffee, but under control), I felt a tentative sense of accomplishment. There was a long road ahead, my debts were still there, my paycheck hadn't magically grown, but I was starting to see the light at the end of the tunnel. Or if not a light, at least a map in my hands for the tunnel.

I crawled into bed, exhausted but content. The workshop, the new friends, the budget, all of it had given me a sense of power over my life that I'd been missing. For the first time since graduation, I felt like maybe I *was* doing this whole adulting thing right or at least getting there.

Tomorrow would bring its challenges, no doubt. But I was meeting them with eyes open and a plan in place. And that felt like a breakthrough indeed.

Chapter 5: The Shackles of Debt

The following week tested my resolve in new ways. Budgeting, I was discovering, wasn't a one-time fix but a daily exercise in self-control. Every decision, from grocery brands to weekend plans, now went through a mental filter: "Can I afford this? Is it in the budget?" It was both empowering and exhausting.

On Wednesday, a small crisis hit: Lisa's car refused to start in the parking lot of the clinic where she worked. By now, we'd all exchanged numbers and even set up a group chat lovingly dubbed "Financial Freedom Fighters" (Kevin's suggestion). So when Lisa sent a flustered voice message about being stranded with her daughter in the backseat, we sprang into action.

As luck would have it, Ray was between jobs that afternoon and offered to drive over to help. "I know a thing or two about cars," he had said. Dante left work a bit early and I tagged along, our boss surprisingly cool with us using some personal hours when we vaguely mentioned "helping a friend with an emergency." (I suspected he thought it was a medical emergency; I decided not to elaborate.)

We found Lisa in the small parking lot behind her clinic, the hood of her aging sedan already propped open by Ray. Marisol was sitting on the curb reading one of her favorite *Baby-Sitters Club* books, seemingly unconcerned by the car malfunction and the crowd surrounding it.

"Thank you guys for coming," Lisa said, looking a bit embarrassed but immensely relieved. "I didn't know who else to call. I was about to phone a tow truck, which I really can't afford..."

"No worries, let's see what's up first," Ray said. He had rolled up his sleeves and was fiddling with the battery cables. "Car just clicked when you turned the key? Not even trying to crank?" he asked.

Lisa nodded. "It was fine this morning, but now it just clicks."

"Might be the battery or a bad alternator." Ray tapped something with a wrench. "Battery terminals are corroded. Hand me that Coke, would ya?"

Dante, who had just bought a can of Coca-Cola from a nearby vending machine for Marisol, looked perplexed. Ray chuckled. "Trust me." He poured a bit of the soda over the white-crusted battery terminals. The acid in the soda fizzed and ate away at the corrosion. After cleaning and tightening the connections, Ray had Lisa try the ignition again. The engine sputtered to life.

"Oh my God!" she exclaimed, covering her mouth, equal parts astonished and delighted. Marisol hopped up, clapping, clearly just happy the car was running so they could go home.

"That should at least get you home," Ray said. "Battery might be on its last legs though. How old is it?"

"Um... five years? Maybe six. I got the car used and never changed it," Lisa admitted.

"Yeah, might need a new one. But don't go to some expensive shop. I can help you get one wholesale and install it. Should save you on labor costs," Ray offered.

Tears sprang in Lisa's eyes, she was the type who felt emotions freely. "You have no idea... I was so scared thinking of the repair bill. I can't thank you enough, Ray." She looked at the rest of us. "All of you. Marisol, what do we say?"

"Thank you!" the little girl chirped.

On the drive back, Dante shook his head in amazement. "I can't believe how everyone jumped in to help. A week ago none of us even knew each other."

"Well, crisis brings people together," I said. "But also, I think we've all just decided to have each other's backs. It's kind of awesome."

It was more than awesome. It was a revelation: financial struggles felt less suffocating when you weren't alone. Lisa likely would have put that car repair on a credit card or, worse, taken out a payday loan had no one been around. Instead, community and a little ingenuity saved the day.

At the session that evening, the theme was tackling debt and avoiding debt traps. It couldn't have been more timely.

Personal Finance Workshop

Session 4 – Breaking the Shackles of Debt

DEBT

Jim started by drawing on the board.

Under it he wrote "Debt" in bold letters. "How many of you feel like debt is holding you back, restrained, confined, like hand cuffs or shackles?" he asked.

All hands went up, including Kevin's, even though he probably had less debt than the rest of us by virtue of youth.

"OK, lets talk about the *shackles of debt*!

Jim then shared a bit of his own story. "In my 20s, I got into credit card trouble, bad. I was trying to keep up with my friends' lifestyles, and before I knew it I had five credit cards all maxed out. Took me years to claw my way out. So, if you're in debt now, believe me, I understand the stress it puts on you. But I also know it's possible to get free of that burden."

He talked about two main strategies: the debt snowball (paying off the smallest balances first to get quick wins and momentum) and the debt avalanche (paying off the highest interest debts first to save money in the long run). "There's no one right method; it depends on what motivates you. Mathematically, avalanche might save a bit more if you stick to it, but psychologically, a lot of people find the snowball approach keeps them going. The key is: you need to pay more than the minimums. If you just pay minimums on credit cards, you'll be in debt for decades in some cases."

He then showed an example on the board, using a hypothetical credit card balance of $5,000 at 18% interest. "If you only pay the minimum, say 2% of balance or $25, you're looking at over 15 years to pay this off and paying almost $5,000 in interest on top of the original $5,000. Financial cuffs like this can really hold you back." We all grimaced.

Sofia raised her hand. "I have a couple of cards and a student loan. Should I prioritize the credit cards because of interest? The student loan interest is lower, but the balance is way higher, so it feels like I'll never finish paying that."

"Great question," Jim replied. "Generally, yes, pay at least the minimum on all to avoid penalties, but throw any extra at the highest interest debt, which is likely your credit cards. Student loans often have lower rates and longer terms, plus sometimes other options like income-based payments. But credit cards can quickly spiral out of control if not reined in."

I nodded, taking notes. I had two credit cards: one with $5,200 at 19.9% (the one I'd been using to float myself recently), and another with $2,000 at 15% that I'd had since college. The smaller one had a lower rate but I was only paying minimums. Under avalanche, I'd tackle the $5,200 first; under snowball, I'd knock out the $2,000 card first. I was leaning towards snowball just for the emotional boost of killing one balance completely. That feeling of accomplishment might keep me motivated.

Kevin spoke up next. "I have one credit card I just got to build credit. Only like a $500 limit. I use it for gas mainly. Is it bad to carry a balance? I heard you need to carry balance to build credit, but also that you shouldn't.

Jim smiled. "There's a lot of myths around credit. The truth is - you build credit by using it responsibly. That means using it a bit and paying it off on time. You don't need to carry a balance and pay interest to improve your credit score. In fact, it's better if you pay in full each month if you can. Your credit utilization ratio, basically the percentage of your credit limit you're using, matters. So if you have a $500 limit and use $100 and pay it off, that's great. If you max it out, that could hurt your score even if you pay it off, depending on the timing. For now, Kevin, just keep doing what you're doing, maybe keep your utilization below 30% of your limit at any time, and pay it off monthly. That will build your credit history fine."

Kevin piped up again. "Is all debt bad? Like, what if I want to get a car loan soon? I've been saving, but not enough to buy outright."

Jim smiled. "Great question, and this is key: not all debt is bad. 'Bad debt' typically includes things like high-interest credit cards, payday loans, or anything spent on items that lose value quickly and don't earn you income. 'Good debt' is usually tied to appreciating assets, like a home mortgage, or investments in yourself, like education or training. A car loan can go either way. Depends on the terms and the car."

Lisa leaned in. "What about leasing? That was offered to me once, but it seemed like a trap."

"It can be," Jim said. "Leasing usually means lower monthly payments, but you don't own the car. There are mileage restrictions and end-of-lease fees. Buying a gently used car and holding onto it can save you thousands in the long run."

Ray nodded. "I always buy used. You let someone else take that big depreciation hit. Plus, I can fix small stuff myself."

We all looked at him like he was a budget magician.

Lisa shifted in her seat. "What about those credit score ads, like checking your score often? Does that hurt your credit? I'm kind of scared to even look at mine after some late bills..." She looked embarrassed, but we all had some dings, I was sure.

"I'm glad you brought this up. Lets dive into credit scores," Jim grabbed a marker as he turned to the board.

Credit Scores

Excellent: 800-850

Very Good: 740-799

Good: 670-739

Fair: 580-669

Poor: 300-579

"These are the credit score ranges," he said. "Higher scores mean lenders trust you more and you'll pay less to borrow. Lower scores? Higher interest rates, or you might get denied."

"Protect it like your reputation. Pay on time, keep balances low, don't open too much new credit. One missed payment can drop your score fast, but building it back up takes time."

He set the marker down. "Treat your score well, and it'll save you thousands over your lifetime. And now I can answer your question Lisa"

"Using free credit score apps or the ones from your bank are typically soft inquiries, they don't hurt your score," Jim said gently. "It's good to check, to know where you stand. And to catch any errors. You can get your full credit report for free annually from each bureau. It's something I'd recommend doing. As for late payments, they do impact your score, unfortunately, especially if over 30 days late. But the more time passes and the more you keep current on everything now, the more your score will recover. We can talk one-on-one about your situation if you want, Lisa."

Darren added, "When I joined the Army, I didn't have any credit history at all. Couldn't even get a basic credit card without my mom co-signing. But she refused, tough love thing. So I had to start with a secured credit card."

Jim nodded. "Yeah, if you've never had a loan or card, you might be 'credit invisible.' You have to build credit from scratch. Secured cards, on-time rent reporting, or credit builder loans are good tools. But co-signing can be risky. If someone misses payments, the co-signer is legally on the hook."

I made a mental note to talk to my younger cousin about that. He was about to ask his mom to co-sign a car loan.

I could see Lisa still worrying; no doubt her single-income life meant some bills likely got paid late in tough times. I made a mental note to check in on her again.

At that point, Darren leaned forward. "You know, credit scores aren't just about getting a loan," he said. "In some jobs, like military intelligence and other sensitive fields, a good credit score can actually be part of the screening process. Agencies want to know you're not in a financial situation where you could be compromised. The military wants to make sure you're not going to sell secrets to the enemy just to get out of debt, for example. So, in some cases, a decent credit score doesn't just help you borrow money, it can help you get, or at least keep, a job."

Lisa's eyes widened. "Wait—you mean my credit could keep me from getting hired somewhere?" she asked, sounding startled.

Jim nodded. "That's a great point, Darren. Credit touches more areas of life than most people realize. It's not just about banks or credit cards—it can affect your housing, your job prospects, even your security clearance in Darren's world. That's why managing debt and building healthy credit habits matters so much." He glanced around the room. "So let's talk about one practical step you can take right now."

He leaned forward. "Has anyone here ever tried to negotiate their debts?" Blank looks. "Believe it or not," he said, "sometimes you can call your credit card company and ask for a lower interest rate, especially if you've been a customer in good standing for a while. They might say no, but worth a try. You can also transfer balances to a card with a 0% intro rate if your credit score allows it, but be careful with those—there are fees, and you need to pay it off before the rate jumps."

He looked at Ray. "Inconsistent income like in construction can be tough for managing debt. One trick is, whenever you get a really good paycheck or contract, try to throw a big chunk at any debt you have, because you might not have that surplus later if work slows. And conversely, in lean times, try at least to pay minimums to avoid fees and hits to your credit, even if you can't pay extra."

Ray nodded. "I usually do that with tax refunds, throw it at the credit card. But then something else always comes up." He sighed. "I'm gonna try the snowball. I owe about $700 on one card and $2,500 on another. If I clear the $700, that'll feel good. Then I'll tackle the bigger one."

As the session went on, I felt a growing determination. When asked, I shared that I planned to wipe out my smaller credit card by the end of the year by cutting more expenses and maybe selling some unused stuff. Saying it out loud made it feel real and achievable.

Dante admitted he had a personal loan for the last bit of his college tuition that he'd been dragging out. "The rate's not too bad, like 6%, but I just kind of forget about it since it's auto-pay. I think I'll try to pay it off early with any bonus I get at work this winter."

Jim clapped his hands once. "That's the spirit. The less debt you carry, the more of your money you get to keep for yourself and your goals. Remember that: every dollar of debt paid off is a dollar you regain freedom over."

Before Jim could move on, Lisa sheepishly raised her hand.

"I have a story," she said, eyes darting around the group. "It's not one I love telling, but maybe it'll help someone."

The room quieted.

"A couple years ago, I was in a really tight spot. My hours had been cut, my rent was due, and I was already behind on my credit card. I didn't want to ask anyone for help, I was embarrassed. So I went to one of those payday loan places."

Sophia winced. Kevin nodded, knowingly.

"They made it sound easy. I could borrow $500, and all I had to do was pay $575 in two weeks. That's just $75 in interest, right? Didn't seem so bad at the time."

She paused. "But I couldn't pay it back in two weeks. So they offered to 'roll it over' into a new loan. That added another $75. Then it happened again. And again."

Maya leaned forward. "Wait… how long did that go on?"

"Three and a half months," Lisa said. "By the time I finally paid it off, I had paid some $525 in fees for that original $500 loan. That's almost 360% annually when you do the math."

The group was silent.

"I felt stupid. Trapped. And worse, I kept it secret. I didn't want anyone to know I couldn't figure things out on my own."

Jim stepped in gently. "Lisa, thank you for sharing that. What you just described is unfortunately really common. Payday loans are marketed as fast fixes, but they're traps. The average payday loan has an APR of **391%**, according to the Consumer Financial Protection Bureau, or CFPB."

He turned back to the board. "This is why we talk about emergency savings and avoiding predatory debt. And it's why understanding your credit options is so important. Because if you don't know your alternatives, you might think this is the only path."

Lisa nodded. "If I had even a few hundred saved, I never would've walked into that place."

Jim then circled back to something often overlooked in budget plans. "One line item people skip, but shouldn't, is giving. Doesn't have to be huge. Could be $10 a month. But regularly giving to causes you care about reminds you that money's not just about survival or getting ahead. It's also about community."

Lisa nodded quietly. "I try to donate to the domestic violence shelter, even if it's just $5 here and there. They helped me a lot once."

Jim was brimming. "That's the spirit, Lisa. Start small and don't wait until your finances "are better" because that time may never come!"

"I wanted to share some stats before we wrap for the day," said Jim as he pulled out his iPhone to look something up. "According to the CFPB the average American carries around $6,000 in credit card debt, and many of those paying only minimums are stuck for over a decade. And if you get hit with medical debt, especially without insurance, those bills can exceed $10,000 or more. Remember Kayla's story? That's how a lot of people end up bankrupt, even while working."

It was a quiet moment. Then Darren said, "That's why I save 20% of everything I earn. Been doing it since basic training. My pops drilled that into me: save before you spend."

"You're my hero," Lisa said with a laugh.

"Seriously," Sofia added. "I'm just trying to save *something* every month."

We all left that night heavy with truth but somehow lighter in spirit. Debt wasn't going to disappear overnight, but for the first time in a long time, it felt like we had a plan. And a team.

By end of class, we each set a specific debt payoff goal:

- I committed to slaying my $2,000 credit card by Christmas.

- Sofia vowed to pay off one of her two cards within 6 months.

- Dante planned to clear his personal loan by spring.

- Ray, as he said, would snowball his smaller card in the next two months.

- Kevin was just going to avoid new debt and pay his card in full (we high-fived him for starting good habits early).

- Lisa, after some hesitation, shared that she wanted to pay off the $1,200 left on a high-interest furniture store credit account she had (from buying a sofa and bed after her divorce) within the next year. It was a burden she hated, she confessed, and that one resonated with me, owing money on something as fundamental as your couch felt like the debt was invading every part of life.

After class, I lingered to ask Jim a question. Dante and Sofia were chatting with Kevin by the snacks, and Lisa had already headed out, needing to get Marisol home for bed.

"Jim, do you think it's worth it for me to try to get another side gig to pay debt faster, or should I focus on cutting expenses?" I asked.

He gave it a moment's thought. "Both, if you have the bandwidth. You're young, so if you can hustle a bit now, you can change your trajectory significantly. Are you looking to add-to or replace your Uber driving income? Austin's got a lot of opportunities for freelance gigs. But don't burn yourself out. Cutting expenses has its limits; earning more has unlimited potential, but also a cost in time and energy. So find a balance. I will say, investing in your career growth to earn a higher salary can pay off the most in the long run. But in the short term, if you want that card gone by Christmas, a side gig for a couple months could get you there."

Kevin then shared something unexpected. "I was gonna buy a new iPad this week. But when I saw my budget, I realized that would wipe out all my savings. I thought about it for a while, and instead I just updated my old laptop and used some of that money to sign up for a course I'd been wanting to take. Felt good. I guess that's opportunity cost, right?"

Jim beamed. "Exactly. Every dollar spent on one thing is a dollar you can't spend elsewhere. That's opportunity cost. What you *don't* buy matters just as much as what you do."

I appreciated Jim's measured take and Kevin's spending constraint. On the drive home, I brainstormed what other side gigs I could do, in addition to, or *instead* of my Uber side hustle. Maybe freelance writing or social media managing for a small business on the side? I had skills from my job that might be marketable. Or delivering groceries - I'd seen plenty of Instacart and Favor delivery folks around.

My phone buzzed as I waited at a red light. A text from Sofia: *"Chicas night soon? Also, I have some clothes & jewelry I never use, thinking to sell online to fund our debt payoff. Want to join? Could be fun photoshoot/sale thing."*

I laughed at her energy. Even dealing with heavy topics, she kept it lighthearted. I texted back: *"I'm in. My closet needs a purge anyway. eBay or Poshmark, here we come."*

That weekend, Sofia and I indeed spent an afternoon digging through our closets, taking photos of gently used dresses, shoes, and accessories we rarely wore. We made a whole event of it, blasting music in her tiny apartment and even roping Kayla in to model a couple of items. By the end, we'd posted dozens of listings for sale. "Even if we make a hundred bucks each, that's going straight to debt!" Sofia declared, high on the productivity.

The momentum kept going over the next month. I found a small freelance gig managing social media for a friend of a friend's bakery on the east side, just a few hours a week in exchange for some extra cash (and the occasional cupcake). It wasn't much, but combined with selling some stuff and tightening my budget, I actually managed to scrape together $500 by mid-November to throw entirely at my credit card. Seeing that balance drop faster than expected was addictive, in the best way.

Not that it was all easy. There were moments of weakness: I nearly caved and bought a new dress I didn't need when I went shopping with a coworker (luckily I put it back after reminding myself of my goals). And I did have a setback when an old cavity flared up, resulting in an unplanned $300 dentist bill that had to go on the credit card. I was frustrated, but instead of throwing up my hands, I adjusted my plan: okay, the card wouldn't be fully paid off by Christmas, but I could still get close.

Our group kept in touch through it all. We met at least once outside of class, like the potluck movie night at my apartment, where Ray indeed brought his famous chili (which was a hit with everyone, including little Marisol, who found it hilarious that we were all eating on a picnic blanket on the floor since my place had limited seating). We watched a library DVD of an old comedy to keep it free and fun. Laughter and the smell of chili filled our home, and not one person spent a dime that night.

By the time the fifth workshop session rolled around, I think all of us felt a little more confident facing our debt dragon. It was still there, breathing fire now and then, but we had our shields and swords, and importantly, we had each other for backup.

Chapter 6: Investing for the Future

The fifth and final official session of the workshop had a buzz of excitement, tinged with a bit of sadness that our structured meetings were coming to an end. Over the past month or so, we'd grown from strangers into something like a team, a motley crew of Austinites united by the quest for financial stability.

Personal Finance Workshop

Session 5 – Investing for the Future

"Welcome back, all. Nice to see your bright shining faces again. Tonight, we're talking about how to make your money work for you," Jim began, beaming at us like a proud teacher on graduation day. He wrote on the board:

Investing & Future Planning

"You've all worked hard on budgeting and tackling debt. Those things help you play defense - protecting your finances. Investing is more like offense - it's how you build wealth over time and reach those big goals."

He drew a timeline on the board, marking points for 5 years, 10 years, 20, 30. "Tell me some goals you might have for the future, small or big."

"Buy a house," Sofia piped up immediately.

"Retire comfortably," Dante added.

"Start my own business," said Ray after a moment of thought.

"Send my kid to college," Lisa said quietly.

"Travel the world," I chimed in, feeling a little shy to admit it out loud. I'd hardly traveled beyond Texas, but it was a dream of mine to see far-off places someday.

Kevin adjusted his UT cap and joked, "Become a millionaire by 30, kidding, kidding." Then more seriously, "I guess... being able to not live paycheck to paycheck and maybe help my parents out."

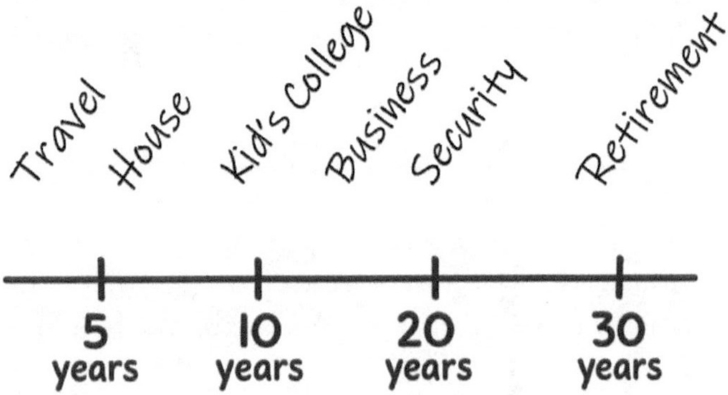

Jim nodded as each of us spoke and jotted words on the timeline: House, Retirement, Business, College for Kid, Travel, Security. "These are wonderful goals. They also generally require money, right? Significant money, in many cases. And that is why learning to invest and save for the future is crucial. Because if you simply stuff cash under a mattress or in a basic checking account, you're likely not even keeping up with inflation, meaning your money loses value over time. But if you invest wisely, your money can grow and multiply."

He then drew what was supposed to resemble a tiny snowball rolling and growing down a hill. Arguably *not* his finest art moment.

"Compound interest," he said, underlining for impact. "This is one of the most powerful forces in finance. It means you earn interest on your money, and then interest on your interest, and so on. Over long periods, it can turn even modest savings into a surprisingly large amount. It's like a snowball rolling downhill, getting bigger all the time."

I leaned forward, already knowing the concept but never having really seen it in action personally. Jim gave an example: "Imagine you put $100 a month into an investment that earns, say, 7% per year on average. In one year you'd have about $1,240 because of the interest. In 10 years, any guesses?"

We shrugged. None of us wanted to do math on the spot.

"Roughly $17,000," Jim smiled.

My eyes widened. $100 a month sounded doable if one was out of debt and earning decently. $17k in ten years from that? Nice.

"And in 20 years? About $50,000. In 40 years, if say Kevin here at 20 started and went until 60, over $250,000, from just that $100 a month."

"Wow," Kevin said, clearly impressed.

Jim took a minute to write a timeless saying on the board:

The best time to plant a tree was 20 years ago. The second-best time is NOW!

"Now imagine if you increase that to $200, $500 a month as your income grows. That's the magic of starting early and being consistent," Jim continued. "For those of us not 20 anymore," he gave a little self-deprecating chuckle, "the next best time to start is now. Even if you can't invest a lot, consistency and time can do wonders. And if you're late to the game, you might just have to save a bit more or work a little longer, but you can still reach your goals with a plan."

Dante raised his hand. "So, what exactly should we be investing in? Like, I hear about stocks and bonds, and I honestly don't really get it. Is it like gambling? I had friends who lost money on those meme stocks last year, and others who swear by crypto... it's confusing."

He wasn't alone; I had the same confusions. I'd heard coworkers throw around terms like "index funds" or complain about their 401(k) performance, but it was like another language to me.

Jim acknowledged our puzzled faces. "Let's break it down simply." He turned to the whiteboard:

Asset Classes

Stocks

Bonds

Real Estate

Mutual Funds

Index Funds

At a high level, you have different asset classes: stocks, bonds, real estate, etc. Stocks mean you're buying a tiny ownership of a company. If the company does well, your stock tends to do well (price goes up, maybe pays dividends). If it does poorly, stock goes down. Bonds are like IOUs, you lend money to a company or government and they pay you interest, generally lower risk and lower return than stocks. Real estate could be owning property or investing through funds. And then there are things like mutual funds or index funds, which are basically baskets of many stocks or bonds, giving you instant diversification."

He paused to ensure we were following, then added, "For most people who are just starting, a good approach is to invest in broad, low-cost index funds or mutual funds, especially in tax-advantaged accounts like a 401(k) or IRA. That way you're not trying to pick individual stocks, which can be risky and time-consuming. Instead, you own a little piece of hundreds of companies. The U.S. stock market historically returns around 7-8% per year on average over decades. Some years it's up, some it's down, but over the long haul it's grown. By being diversified, you ride the overall growth instead of betting on a few winners or losers."

Jim paused to drive the point home. "And we're talking long-term investing here, not day trading," he said firmly. "Some folks treat the stock market like a casino, chasing hot stocks or trying to time every rise and fall. But for ordinary people like us, the real power is in steady, consistent investing and letting time do the heavy lifting. It might not be flashy, but it works."

Sofia raised a concern. "What about risk? Like, my parents lost a lot in the 2008 crash. They had to postpone retirement. I'm afraid of that happening."

Jim gave a sympathetic nod. "Market crashes do happen. 2008 was a big one, and there was another dip in 2020 when the pandemic hit, though that one recovered quickly. The key is not to panic and not to invest money you need in the short term. If your timeline for the goal is long, like retirement or a house you plan to buy in 10 years, you can ride out those ups and downs. If you stay invested, historically the market recovers and then some. Those who sold at the bottom locked in losses. Those who hung on or even bought more when things were low ended up okay when the market bounced back. It's easier said than done emotionally, of course." He then returned to the board with one of his illustrations:

Stocks Over Time

Jim then continued, "The entire stock market goes up and down, as do individual stocks. Historically the market has always recovered, but you never know when its going to reverse course. This is good news for those with a long time horizon, but potentially risky for those who might need to pull their investments earlier. An investment today in an index fund that tracks the S&P 500, a group of 500 of the leading companies, is almost surely going to be worth more in 20 years. However, on a shorter time frame, 10 and 5 years, there's a decent chance that the value actually goes down. In 1 year the chances of the value dropping are very high."

"Before making any investment," he continued, "be sure to know your time horizon. The worst thing to do is to buy a stock today and then sell it as soon as the value goes down because the investor gets scared about losing their money. You only lose when you sell for less than you paid. Holding a stock position through the ups and downs of normal market fluctuations is the best way to make your money grow."

Kevin, who had been scribbling notes, looked up. "This might be a dumb question, but what's an ETF? I see that term on Reddit and stuff. Is that like an index fund?"

Jim started to respond, but Darren surprisingly stepped in with a quiet confidence. "I can answer that," he said. All eyes turned to Darren, who had mostly listened until now. "ETF stands for Exchange-Traded Fund. It's basically a mutual fund that trades like a stock. Index funds can come in the form of traditional mutual funds or ETFs. The main difference is that an ETF can be bought or sold throughout the trading day on a stock exchange, whereas a mutual fund is priced just once at the end of the day." He spoke clearly, in plain language. "For example, you could buy an S&P 500 index as a mutual fund or as an ETF. Either way, you're getting the same basket of 500 companies. But the ETF you can trade at 10am or 2pm or whenever the market's open, just like you'd trade a share of Apple or Tesla. Mutual funds, you place an order and you get whatever the closing price is at end of day."

Kevin nodded along. "So they're basically the same thing inside, just the way you buy and sell is different?"

"Exactly," said Darren. "ETFs often have very low fees too, and you can start with just the price of one share which might be, say, $50 or $100, whereas some mutual funds might require a minimum like $1,000 to start. But many index mutual funds have low minimums these days too. The key point is both ETFs and mutual funds let you invest in lots of stuff at once easily."

Jim was smiling as Darren spoke, clearly pleased to see peer knowledge-sharing. Darren went on, "I've been investing mostly in index funds and index ETFs for years. For my retirement account, I use something similar to a 401(k) for military folks, and it mostly goes into broad index funds. I don't mess with picking individual stocks too much, just a few small ones here and there for fun, because I'd rather not risk it. The bulk of my money, I keep it diversified and steady."

Kevin looked relieved at Darren's straightforward explanation. "Got it. That makes sense. Thank you."

Jim gave an approving nod. "Great explanation, Darren. And Kevin, there are no dumb questions here. ETFs, mutual funds, index funds, what matters is they're tools to help regular people invest without needing to be stock-picking experts. As Darren said, the big benefit is diversification and low cost."

Ray raised his hand tentatively. "I'm still a bit fuzzy," he admitted. "Is an index fund basically the same as an ETF, or something different?"

Jim was happy to clarify. "Good question. 'Index fund' just means a fund designed to track a market index, like the S&P 500. It can come in the form of a mutual fund or an ETF. For example, there's the S&P 500 index as a mutual fund and also as an ETF, they both hold the same 500 companies. The key is that index funds are passive, meaning they just mirror the market, and they usually have very low fees. On the other hand, some mutual funds are actively managed. That means a manager is picking stocks and trying to beat the market. Those often charge higher fees. And truth is, over the long run, most of those active funds don't outperform the simple index funds, especially after you account for fees."

Ray nodded as that sank in. "So, sticking with low-cost index funds is usually the way to go?"

Jim smiled. "Often, yes. For most of us, keeping it simple with index funds or broad ETFs is a solid approach. It's not about trying to outsmart the market, it's about getting the market's growth working for you."

Darren tapped his pen on his notepad and chimed in quietly, "That's basically what I do, too. Keeps it simple, and it works."

Dante leaned forward, intrigued. "All that makes sense about funds," he said. "But what if we *do* want to try buying a stock or two ourselves? Any tips on doing that without, you know, losing our shirts?"

Darren cracked a rare smile and straightened up. "I'm no expert stock guru," he began, "but I've learned a few things. First, I only buy stocks in companies I actually understand and believe have a good future. And I never put too much money into one stock, just an amount I'm okay with risking. Individual stocks can be a rollercoaster, so you don't want your rent money riding on one company.

Second, do your homework before you buy. Look at what the company does, maybe skim their financials or read some news about them. Don't just buy something because it's hyped on Reddit or a friend gave you a hot tip. I made that mistake when I started, I jumped on a 'hot' stock without really knowing anything about it, and I ended up buying near its peak. It tanked and I panicked and sold at a loss. Learned my lesson there." He shook his head at the memory.

"Now, I try not to let emotions control me. If a stock I own drops but nothing major has changed with the company itself, I hold on or even consider buying more. If it shoots up really fast, sometimes I'll sell a little and enjoy the gain. Basically, I set some rules for myself so I don't buy or sell just because everyone else is."

He glanced around at us and added, "And honestly, I keep those individual stock bets pretty small, like the fun part of my portfolio. The majority of my money is still in the diversified index funds for the long haul. That way, if one of my stock picks goes south, it stings a little but it doesn't derail my overall plan."

Dante let out a breath and nodded. "Thanks, man. Good to know. No YOLO bets for me," he said, referencing the slang for risky all-in trades that had made the rounds online. We all chuckled.

Jim looked pleased that we were learning from each other.

Jim continued, "So you manage risk by diversifying, owning many different investments, maybe some international stocks too, not just U.S., maybe some bonds which are steadier, etc., and by adjusting as you get closer to needing the money. For example, I was more aggressive with my investments in my 30s and 40s. Now that I'm late 50s, I've shifted some money to bonds and cash because I can't afford to lose a big chunk right before retirement. You young folks have more time to recover, so you can take more risk if you’re comfortable with it."

It was a lot to absorb, but hearing it conversationally helped demystify it.

Before moving on, Jim recapped what he called the basic "investing commandments" for us. He raised five fingers and went through them one by one: "First, start as early as you can and invest consistently. Second, diversify your investments, don't put all your money in one stock or one thing. Third, think long-term; avoid trying to time the market or day-trade on hot tips. Fourth, keep your costs low, like using low-fee index funds and ETFs. And fifth, stay disciplined and stick to your plan, don't let fear or greed make you buy or sell at the wrong times."

We all nodded as he spoke, each principle reinforcing the mindset we'd been building over the past weeks.

"One more thing," Jim said, underlining the phrase Tax-Advantaged on the whiteboard.

Tax-Advantaged

"Make sure to take advantage of things like employer retirement plans or IRAs. Maya, Dante, does your employer offer a 401(k) or anything?"

I felt a little flush of guilt. "Uh, yes, we have a 401(k) at work. There's a 3% matching too. But I've only been contributing like $50 a month because I felt I needed every dollar in my paycheck. I realize that's probably a mistake." Especially hearing about free matching money, an older colleague had scolded me once for leaving that on the table.

Dante jumped in, "Same here. I've been meaning to start contributing. They auto-enrolled me at 3% when I got hired, but I opted out because I thought I'd rather pay my loans first. Now I'm thinking I should at least do enough to get the match."

Jim smiled. "Getting the employer match is usually a no-brainer, it's effectively free money or an instant 100% return on your contribution. So if you can, contribute at least that much. Beyond that, whether you prioritize extra investing versus debt payoff can depend on interest rates and personal preference. But I'd say high-interest debt like credit cards should be killed off before you invest heavily. Lower interest debt like student loans, you might do in parallel with starting to invest for retirement. It's a balance."

Jim capped off the investing talk with retirement accounts. "Let's talk about IRAs," he said, while writing on the board:

IRA = Individual Retirement Account

"If your employer doesn't offer a retirement plan or even if they do and you want to save more, you can open an IRA on your own. There are two main types: Traditional and Roth. With a Traditional IRA, you might get a tax deduction now for what you contribute, but you'll pay taxes later when you withdraw in retirement. A Roth IRA is the opposite: you contribute money you've already paid tax on, and later in retirement you can take it out completely tax-free."

My eyes lit up. The idea of tax-free money in the future sounded pretty great.

Lisa raised her hand. "So, is one type better than the other?" she asked.

Jim shrugged lightly. "It depends on your situation. If you're young or not making a ton of money yet, a Roth IRA is often a great choice. You pay taxes now while you're in a lower bracket, and then all that money grows tax-free. By the time you retire, you don't owe a dime in taxes on it. On the other hand, if you need the tax break now or think you'll be in a much lower tax bracket when you retire, a Traditional IRA could be useful. Some people even split between both. The important thing is that you save something for retirement."

Kevin was practically bouncing in his seat. "I'm definitely going Roth," he announced. "I don't earn much at my part-time job, so it makes sense to get taxed on that now and let it grow."

Jim grinned at Kevin's enthusiasm. "Good call. As long as you have some earned income, you can contribute. Even if it's just $50 a month, starting now will pay off big time down the road."

I made a note to myself to look into opening a Roth IRA too, after hearing all this. Sofia was nodding thoughtfully; it seemed we were all considering how to fit retirement savings into our plans.

We also touched on other future planning aspects:

Emergency funds – aiming eventually for 3-6 months of essential expenses saved.

Health insurance – ensuring we all had health coverage (we did, thankfully; either through work or, in Lisa's case, through a state program for her child and an affordable plan for herself). I couldn't help but think of Kayla and her cautionary tale. She will never be uninsured again and nor should we.

Life insurance – if people depended on our income. None of us carried life insurance yet, though Jim gently pointed out that Lisa might consider a small policy since she had Marisol depending on her.

Estate planning basics – like having a will. Jim said this was important for all adults, regardless of age, net worth, or family status. Wills primarily specify what to do with your assets (money, accounts, property, etc.) once you pass away, but they also include provisions for guardianship and other wishes. A lot of people don't want to even think about these things, it's understandably a sad topic, but if you don't plan for it, your wishes may not be carried out. Or worse, the burden of making tough decisions falls on those you leave behind.

As the session drew to a close, Jim glanced at the clock and clapped his hands together. "Before we wrap up, let's do one last exercise," he said, reaching into his folder. He pulled out the net worth worksheets we'd filled out on day one and passed them around. "Time to update these numbers. Even if the changes are small, it's important to track your progress."

We all hunched over our sheets, recalculating. A few minutes later, Sofia broke the silence. "Guys, my credit card debt is down by $300 from when we started!" she blurted out, eyes shining. "I know it's not huge but seeing that number drop feels so good."

Ray grinned, "I sold my old guitar and put $500 of that toward my car loan. My net worth is still negative," he chuckled, "but hey, it's about $500 less in the red now."

Dante nodded, "I've been chipping away at my student loans. I managed to pay an extra $200 this month. It's a small dent, but it's something."

Lisa spoke softly, but her smile was big. "I finally started an emergency fund. There's $250 in it. I've never had savings before, so... I'm pretty proud of that." We all applauded quietly for her, and I saw Lisa blink back a tear of happiness.

Kevin practically bounced in his seat. "I saved up $100 and even invested some of it!" he said proudly. "A month ago I had nothing set aside."

I looked down at my own worksheet, hardly believing the difference a few weeks made. By cutting back on my takeout and sticking to the budget, I'd paid off $400 on my smallest credit card and added about $200 to my savings. My net worth was still below zero, but it was creeping upward for the first time ever.

Net Worth = Assets - Liabilities			
Assets		**Liabilities**	
401(k)	$3,310	Credit Cards	$6,800
Investments	$1,000	Student Debt	$23,750
Savings	$200		
Total	$4,510	Total	$30,550
Net Worth =	**-$26,040**		

"This is how it starts," Jim said, nodding at all of us with a broad smile. "Little by little. I'm so proud of you all. Remember these wins and keep going. Update your net worth regularly, monthly, every few months, whatever works, to keep yourself motivated. You've seen that progress is possible."

We felt a collective glow of accomplishment. In less than two months, our numbers had begun to move in the right direction. More importantly, our mindset had shifted. We knew we could do this.

By the end of the session, Jim had essentially given us a road map for the rest of our financial journey, which he wrote on the last clean section of whiteboard:

Your Roadmap

Get debt-free

Build savings

Invest for the future consistently

Protect yourself with insurance

and keep learning

He passed around a sheet titled "Next Steps & Resources" with a list of books, websites, and local organizations. I recognized a couple of book titles from what I'd seen online or had recommended to me, including:

- *The Psychology of Money* by Morgan Housel
- *The Wealthy Gardener* by John Soforic
- *The Millionaire Next Door* by Thomas J. Stanley and William D. Danko
- and *The Financial Empowerment Handbook* by David Gatchell.

When it was time to wrap up, none of us wanted to leave. We lingered, thanking Jim profusely for all his guidance. He gave each of us a firm handshake (and Lisa a hug, because she was getting teary-eyed again and insisted).

"You've all got what it takes to succeed," he told us, voice a bit thick with emotion himself. "I'm proud of the progress you've made while we've been together. Please keep in touch, let me know how you're doing, and if you ever have a question or just want to chat, I'm a phone call or email away. Once a teacher, always a teacher, I guess."

We promised we would. In fact, Sofia had already suggested we have a little graduation celebration of our own. So that Friday we all met at a popular food truck park in East Austin to celebrate.

It was a crisp evening with strings of lights twinkling overhead and the smells of various cuisines in the air. We chose this spot because it was budget-friendly and very Austin. Everyone was there, Kevin even brought his girlfriend, a shy biology major, and Dante brought along one of our coworkers (platonically, just to include more people). Kayla joined too, since she was an honorary member by proxy.

We pooled tables together and shared an eclectic feast: tacos al pastor, brisket sandwiches, Thai fried rice, and some vegan tofu tacos that Sofia swore by. The mood was festive. And the best part: no guilt. We had all budgeted for this outing days in advance, agreeing to set aside maybe $15-$20 each for a fun night out. It felt so good to spend within my plan, enjoyment without the aftertaste of worry.

At one point, with paper plates cleared and a second round of Topo Chico sparkling waters opened (we skipped the pricey beers, mostly), I raised my bottle. "I want to propose a toast, uh, even if it's just mineral water."

Everyone laughed and clinked their bottles or cups with mine.

"To us," I said. "For taking control of our lives and for not letting money problems hold us back. And to the friendships we've made along the way. I honestly couldn't have done it without you all." My eyes darted to each face, Sofia, Dante, Ray, Lisa, Kevin, and lingered on Jim, whom we had convinced to join as well. "And especially to Jim, for being our guide."

"Hear, hear!" Dante shouted as we all cheered and took a swig.

Jim looked a little embarrassed but pleased. "Thank you. But really, it's all you. I'm honored to have been part of your journey. Keep it up, and in a few years, I'll be coming to you for advice!"

During a lull, Lisa exclaimed. "I have something to show you all," she said, digging into her purse. She pulled out a certificate and put it on the table. It was an enrollment confirmation: she had signed up for evening classes at Austin Community College to become a certified dental hygienist.

Her eyes shone as she explained, "Watching you go through the job search and seeing all you've achieved... it inspired me. I love my clinic, but reception pay will never be great. As a hygienist, I can triple my salary. It'll be a lot of work studying at night and weekends for two years, but Marisol is behind me and I want to build a better life for us. So... I'm doing it!"

I nearly squealed and put my arm around her. "Lisa, that's amazing! You'll be awesome. And we'll help with whatever you need. Study sessions, watching Marisol occasionally, anything. I'm so proud of you!"

We spent the rest of the night talking about anything and everything, upcoming holidays, funny stories from our jobs, even our families. We were solidifying bonds that felt like they'd last beyond the workshop.

As I drove home with Kayla afterward, I realized this ending was really a beginning. We had finished the classes, sure, but the real story of our financial lives was just getting started. We had plans now: concrete, exciting plans. I was going to up my 401(k) contribution to get the full match starting with my next paycheck. Sofia had opened a Roth IRA with the help of a friend who worked at a bank. Dante was already researching MBA programs and plotting how to balance that with work in a year or two. Ray had set up an appointment with a credit counselor Jim recommended, to explore maybe buying a modest home in Pflugerville where prices were lower, he'd never thought it possible until now. Lisa had started a small side business baking custom birthday cakes on weekends, the money from which went straight into a savings account for Marisol.

And Kevin, dear eager Kevin, had not only opened a Roth IRA through an online brokerage and started investing $50 a month, but he was also spreading the gospel, he'd convinced two of his roommates to join the next personal finance workshop series.

We might not meet every Tuesday at the library anymore, but we had our group chat and budding friendships. In fact, we'd already penciled in a check-in meeting a month out to see how our finances were looking (planning to update our net worth numbers again) and cook another potluck. Accountability at its finest.

Things were looking up, and I felt a swell of gratitude as I pulled into my apartment parking lot. Gratitude for knowledge, for support, and for the city around me that somehow brought us all together. Austin felt a little more like home than it ever had.

Little did I know that soon life would throw one more curveball our way, a test of how far I'd really come on this journey. But that night, under the stars of a Texas sky, with laughter still echoing in my ears, I was ready for whatever came next.

Chapter 7: A Holiday on a Budget

The first real test of my new financial lifestyle came with the holiday season. December blew into Austin with a rare chill – as if the universe knew we needed a little extra willpower to avoid splurging on seasonal lattes and shopping sprees. The city twinkled with lights and decorations, and every other billboard or ad seemed to shout about holiday sales and must-have gifts.

In the past, Christmas had been both joyful and stressful for me. I loved the festivities, but the expectation of gifts and travel usually meant swiping my credit card and worrying about it later. I'd usually spend the first few months of the new year digging myself out of the debt I racked up each December. This year, I vowed, would be different. I wasn't going to undo all my hard-won progress for a few weeks of extravagance.

Our group decided to tackle the holidays as a team. In early December, we gathered at Sofia's apartment – which was cheerfully decked out with paper snowflakes made by her students and a tiny Christmas tree she'd bought on clearance last January. Over hot cocoa (made with store-brand mix, as she proudly noted), we laid out a holiday game plan. For once, we were being proactive, mapping out how to celebrate without breaking the bank instead of just bracing for impact. It felt empowering to brainstorm together and anticipate potential budget-busters before they happened.

"Let's set ground rules for gifts," Dante suggested, pulling out a notepad and clicking his pen. "We could do Secret Santa so we each only buy one gift, and put, like, a $20 limit on it."

"$20? How about $10?" Sofia shot back, pushing her glasses up as she got excited. "We can get creative with it. Maybe even thrift something or make something by hand."

"I love that. Thrifting a gift is like a treasure hunt," Kevin agreed.

Lisa exhaled in relief and managed a smile. "Only having to buy one small gift instead of five or six... honestly, that's a huge relief."

Sofia was indeed crafty – she had already knitted a scarf for her mom using yarn remnants – so we all knew homemade gifts were right up her alley. In the end, we agreed: one Secret Santa gift each, max $10-$15 value, with homemade or secondhand strongly encouraged. We wrote everyone's name on slips of paper and tossed them in a cereal bowl. There was laughter and a little good-natured jostling as we each drew a name. I picked Kevin's name and immediately started brainstorming a "starter finance kit" for him, maybe a budget planner and a goofy piggy bank as a gag. By the grin on Dante's face when he peeked at his slip, I could tell he had something clever in mind, too. When Lisa unfolded her paper and realized she'd gotten me, she just pressed a finger to her lips with a grin – not about to spoil any surprises.

With gifts sorted out, we turned to planning a low-cost holiday party for ourselves. Instead of an expensive night out or restaurant dinner, we would have a cozy potluck meal at my apartment (it was the most central location). Each person volunteered to bring a dish, which not only spread out the work and cost, but also gave us a fun mix of our families' holiday traditions.

"I can make tamales," Ray offered immediately. "Homemade tamales are cheap but labor intensive, so consider it my gift to y'all." He wiggled his eyebrows, and we all cheered at the idea of authentic tamales on the menu.

"I'll do my mom's famous arroz con leche," Sofia said. "It's basically rice, milk, and sugar – super cheap, and you guys know how good it is." We did; her arroz con leche was legendary from past potlucks.

Dante raised his hand next. "I've got a turkey breast in my freezer that I snagged at 40% off in a post-Thanksgiving sale. I'll figure out how to season and roast it, YouTube hasn't failed me yet." He looked both confident and a little nervous, which made us laugh.

"I'll handle sides," I said. "Kayla already offered to help me chop and prep. I'm thinking roasted veggies and mashed potatoes – inexpensive crowd-pleasers. We can probably feed everyone for just a few dollars each on those."

Lisa bounced Marisol on her knee. "And I'll bring a punch – non-alcoholic but festive. It's my Tía Rosa's hibiscus and cinnamon recipe. I can make a huge batch for just a few bucks, and Marisol can have some, too."

In no time, we had a full holiday feast planned out. "Let's see," I murmured, scribbling rough numbers on Dante's notepad. "If each of us spends maybe $10 or so on our dish, the whole dinner will cost under $60 total. That's like $10 each for a feast!" I looked up at our group around Sofia's coffee table. "We'd spend five times that at a restaurant for a holiday meal."

"Way better and way more special," Sofia agreed, clinking her mug of cocoa against mine. It was hard not to feel a swell of pride – we were turning the season of excessive spending into something personal, affordable, and fun.

As we sipped our cocoa, I wondered aloud, "So, what about other holiday plans? Family visits, events – how are you all handling those on a budget?"

Sofia sighed, glad I asked. "My sisters are flying in to visit and they keep wanting to do expensive dinners and outings. I love spending time with them, but I just don't have the cash for fancy steakhouses or $40 brunches right now."

"Why not suggest some alternatives?" I offered. "Austin has the Trail of Lights at Zilker Park. It's just a few bucks donation, and some nights are free. We could all go together – it's really fun to walk through the displays. Or drive around and see neighborhood Christmas lights with hot chocolate in a thermos. That's completely free and still festive."

Her eyes lit up as I talked. "You know, that's a great idea! They might actually love that. And maybe I can host a game night at my place for them one evening instead of us going out on the town. I'll make some snacks, we can play cheesy holiday charades or something. They'll just have to understand I'm on a budget this year."

"Honestly, if they don't get it, that's on them," Dante said. "You're being responsible. Who knows, maybe you'll inspire them to save a little money too."

It struck me then how all of us were learning to communicate our financial boundaries. It wasn't always easy, there's guilt, and the fear of missing out can tug at you when everyone else seems to be splurging, but having each other made us feel less alone in setting those limits.

As the conversation lulled, Lisa had been quiet, biting her lip. I noticed her staring down at her cocoa, lost in thought. Finally, she took a breath and spoke softly. "I want to make Christmas really special for Marisol, but money is so tight..." Her voice quavered, and we all turned our attention to her. "I've picked up a few small things for her over the past months – a used dollhouse I found at Goodwill and repainted, some art supplies from the dollar store – but she's been writing letters to Santa about this fancy kids' tablet that some of her classmates have. There's just no way I can afford that. I hate the thought of her feeling disappointed on Christmas morning." Lisa's eyes brimmed with tears that she quickly brushed away. "I feel like I'm failing her."

Immediately, Sofia scooted closer and put an arm around Lisa. "Hey, you're an amazing mom, first of all. Marisol has so much love in her life, that counts way more than expensive gadgets."

"And Santa can get pretty creative," Dante added gently. "Maybe he leaves her a special letter instead of the tablet. He could say he's proud of her for being such a good girl and maybe set up a fun scavenger hunt around the house for her other little gifts. Kids remember the magical little experiences, not the price tag of a present."

I snapped my fingers as an idea struck. "You know, I actually have some cute accessories left over from an old tablet I don't use anymore – a sparkly case, some stickers, little headphones with cat ears. What if Santa delivers those to Marisol, with a note like, 'I'll bring the tablet when you're a bit older; for now, enjoy these goodies'? That way it feels like part of a promise for the future."

Lisa wiped a tear and managed a genuine smile. "I love that. She might actually find that really cool, like a tease for what's to come. Thank you." She looked around at all of us. "Really, thank you. I just... I hate that I can't give her everything she asks for."

"It's not silly to feel that way," I said, squeezing her hand. "We all want to spoil the people we love during the holidays. But think of it this way, by keeping things modest, we're also teaching our kids, and ourselves, something important about not overspending."

Sofia nodded. "Right. Maybe Marisol won't get the tablet now, but she's getting a mom who doesn't have to work extra hours or stress out because of holiday debt. That is a gift, too."

"And just wait," I added with a grin. "At the rate you're going, by next Christmas you'll be in a much better place financially. Who knows, maybe by then Santa really *will* have a tablet for her under the tree." I gave Lisa a little wink.

Lisa laughed and rubbed her eyes. "Next year," she agreed, her voice full of hope. "Next year will be even better."

With our game plan set and everyone feeling more optimistic, we wrapped up that meeting in good spirits. Walking home, I realized I felt something unfamiliar: I wasn't dreading the holiday season at all. In fact, I was looking forward to it.

Meanwhile, I had my own family to think about, too. I was planning to visit my mom in San Antonio for Christmas. In past years, I'd guiltily splurged on expensive gifts for her, fancy gadgets, jewelry, trying to make up for not visiting as often, or maybe to prove that my post-college "real job" meant I could shower her with the kind of things she never bought for herself. But Mom didn't need or even want those fancy things. This year, I decided I'd do something more meaningful and budget friendly.

Over the first couple of weeks of December, I put together a photo album of my life in Austin to give her – pictures of my apartment, the university campus where I spent time, and my friends. I even included snapshots of our little finance group (I knew Mom would get a kick out of the fact that one of my friends, Ray, could make tamales just like she could). Alongside the album, I wrote her a long, heartfelt letter telling her how much her sacrifices meant to me and how she'd inspired me to keep going even when things were hard. The only store-bought item I added was a warm shawl I found on clearance – I remembered her shivering during her last visit since she never seems to buy anything cozy for herself. Printing the photos and buying the shawl cost a little money, but overall this gift was more about time and thought than dollars.

When I traveled home for Christmas, I went armed with all my new frugal tricks. I carpooled with a friend who was driving to San Antonio, which cut our gas expense in half. I set a firm limit on trip expenses by carrying only the cash I'd budgeted for, leaving my credit cards tucked away. I brought snacks for the road instead of hitting drive-thrus, and I avoided the siren call of those last-minute "convenience" gifts at highway rest stops and gas stations. (In the past I was guilty of grabbing extra stocking stuffers or pointless souvenirs during the drive, just because they were there.) Not this time.

Christmas at Mom's was simple and lovely. We spent Christmas Eve cooking a big dinner together – or rather, I cooked while insisting that she relax in the living room.

"Ay, mija, you work so hard. Let me do the cooking," Mom protested when I shooed her away from the stovetop.

"No way, Mama," I said, gently guiding her to sit down. "Tonight I'm the chef and you are the guest. My only job is making sure you take it easy for once."

She chuckled and finally relented, wrapping herself in a blanket on the couch while I made us a modest but delicious meal of roast chicken, vegetables, and her favorite rice pudding for dessert. I had picked up all the ingredients at the grocery store earlier with cash, and for once I didn't flinch at the total or secretly panic – I actually had a little cushion in my bank account for holiday expenses, planned out in advance. It felt good to offer, "Mom, let me cover the groceries for Christmas dinner," and know that I could do it without any stress.

When we exchanged gifts that night, I was practically bouncing with excitement for her to open hers. I handed Mom the wrapped album and the letter I'd tied with a ribbon, and watched as she carefully peeled back the paper.

She flipped open the photo album and immediately gasped. On the first page was a picture of me standing in front of my little Austin apartment, grinning ear to ear. "Oh, Maya," she murmured, "look at you." As she turned each page, her face lit up at some pictures and crumpled in happy tears at others. There was one of me and my friends posing with a snowman we'd made during a rare Austin snow day; another of Ray and me in his kitchen, holding up a platter of tamales triumphantly. "Dios mío, he even looks like he knows what he's doing with those tamales!" she laughed, wiping her eyes.

By the time she got to the back of the album, where I had tucked in my letter, Mom was openly crying. She read my handwritten pages in silence. Then she removed her glasses, set them on the table, and pulled me into the tightest hug. "This is the best gift I could have asked for, mija," she said softly into my hair. I felt her tears on my cheek, and my own eyes were damp too.

"Read the last page," I whispered, gently disentangling to point at the letter where I'd written a final note.

She picked up the letter again and read the part where I thanked her for always being in my corner and promised that I was finally getting my life together financially. Her chin trembled as she finished the letter. ""I'm so proud of you, Maya," she managed. You're so smart and thoughtful now."

I gave her the shawl next, wrapping it around her thin shoulders. "For those chilly Texas nights," I joked.

Mom ran her fingers over the soft fabric. It was a deep teal color that looked beautiful on her. "You remembered I get cold," she said, smiling through her tears. She stood up and did a little twirl with the shawl like it was a fancy cape. "My daughter, the responsible one, buying things on sale and making me cry with a letter," she teased, laughing as she dabbed at her eyes again.

We spent the next hour curled up on the sofa, looking through the album again together. I told her the story behind each photo, how Kevin had drawn a caricature of me in one of my classes and that picture was tucked in the album; how Lisa's little girl had insisted I include a selfie of the two of us making funny faces; how Dante and I had completed a 5K run (mostly walking, truth be told) which is why we looked so exhausted but proud in that one picture. Mom hung on every word. It struck me that this was the least expensive gift I'd ever given her, yet it was probably the one she appreciated most.

The next morning, as Mom was tidying up wrapping paper remnants and I was savoring a cup of coffee, I noticed a stack of unopened bills and statements piled on a shelf near the kitchen door. They looked like they'd been sitting there a while. I knew money was always tight for Mom, and I suddenly remembered my promise to myself to help her if I could. My stomach fluttered with nerves, I didn't want to pry or make her feel bad, but I mustered my courage.

"Mom," I asked gently, "would you want to go over some of your bills together? Maybe we can come up with a simple budget or something, like I've been doing for myself."

She glanced over at the pile of envelopes and sighed. "Ay, I know I should, but... I get so overwhelmed, mija. I've been avoiding those." She hesitated, looking a little embarrassed. "I'm not as organized as you. I always admired that about you, you know," she added, to my surprise.

I nearly snorted into my coffee, me, organized? That was a first. A few months ago I was a financial mess. But I realized in her eyes, I had started to get it together, and she was proud of that. "I wasn't very organized before," I admitted, "but I've learned a few tricks. How about we try it? Two heads are better than one."

She gave a little nod, almost sheepish. "Okay. I'd like that."

We spent the next couple of hours at the kitchen table, turning that intimidating stack of bills into something she could manage. I fetched my notebook and a calculator, and we opened each envelope one by one.

"Let's list out everything," I said, drawing columns. "Income on one side, all the monthly expenses on the other."

Her income was pretty fixed: Social Security and a small check from the church daycare where she helped out a few mornings a week. Then we wrote down her expenses: the mortgage (thankfully almost paid off, but not quite), utilities, groceries, medications, tithes to church, and the minimum payments on her credit card. I tried not to wince when I saw the credit card balance, clearly, a lot of necessities had ended up on there over time.

"I usually pay the most important things first," Mom said, watching as I penciled in numbers, "and if I can't cover something, well... it waits." She looked down at her hands. "I know that's not good. I just hate seeing the total. It's like if I don't look, I can pretend it's not so bad."

I put my hand over hers. "I used to do the same thing," I told her softly. "Remember how I wouldn't even open my credit card bills right after college?" She nodded. "But it actually feels better to know. Even if the numbers aren't great, at least you can plan. We'll figure it out together, okay?"

We went through each expense. I showed her how I track my due dates so I don't miss any payments. We even set up her electric and water bills to auto-pay through the utility company so she wouldn't accidentally miss a month and get hit with late fees. I marked the due dates for her mortgage and credit card on a big wall calendar she had hanging by the fridge.

She was a quick learner once she got past the initial fear. "You make it seem simple," she said, sounding a little surprised.

"It *is* simpler when it's all on one page," I smiled, showing her the completed budget in my notebook. We had managed to find a small amount, just a sliver of her income, left over each month. "See this? This $50 is unassigned. We could put that toward your credit card or set it aside for an emergency."

"Maybe emergencies," Mom said after a moment. "I hate using that card, and I only do when I have to. If I have a little savings, maybe I won't need it as much."

I nodded enthusiastically. "Exactly." Honestly, I was amazed. Here was my mom, who had always handled money privately, actually letting me in and taking my advice. It felt incredible to be able to help her, even if I couldn't magically fix the fact that her income was small. At least now she had a clearer picture of her finances, and a plan.

We even talked about her ditching the expensive check-cashing place she sometimes used. When Mom mentioned she often went there because it was walking distance and she didn't trust big banks after a bad experience years ago, I had an idea. "Mom, there's a local credit union two blocks from the grocery store. They're really community-focused and have low fees. I bet we could set you up with a free checking account there, so you wouldn't lose money every time you cash a check or pay a bill."

She raised her eyebrows. "Really? They won't charge an arm and a leg? I tried a bank when I first moved here, but they kept charging me fees I didn't understand."

"I promise, a credit union is different. We can ask all the questions you want. How about we go tomorrow morning and talk to them? I'll come with you."

She mulled it over and then nodded. "Yes. Tomorrow."

The next day, I drove Mom to the neighborhood credit union. The difference was night and day from her old bank experience, one of the representatives even spoke Spanish and switched to it when she noticed Mom struggling with some of the paperwork. In less than an hour, Mom had opened a free checking account (with no minimum balance requirement) and a savings account. They even set her up with a debit card. When we walked out, Mom was holding the little envelope with her new debit card inside like it was some fragile treasure.

"No more crazy check-cashing fees, eh, Mom?" I teased, giving her a side hug.

She actually laughed. "I feel like a weight's been lifted. Thank you, mija." She squeezed my hand. It was a subtle role reversal: for so long, she'd taken care of me, and now I had helped take care of her. I realized I could get used to this feeling, being able to give back to the woman who had given me so much.

That afternoon, we treated ourselves to a cup of coffee at her kitchen table, both of us feeling lighter. As we sat there, Mom grew quiet, staring into her mug as if gathering courage for something.

"There's someone I want to tell you about," she began slowly. "You know Rosa, right? My friend from church who used to sing in the choir?"

I nodded. I remembered Rosa, she was a kindly older woman who always had a peppermint in her purse for the kids and a warm hug for me whenever I visited home. "Sure, I remember Rosa. How is she?"

Mom sighed and looked down. "She... well, last year she had to go back to work. At sixty-eight years old."

I nearly dropped my coffee. "Wait, she un-retired? At 68? Why? I thought she and her husband were finally going to relax and enjoy life."

"They thought so too," Mom said, shaking her head sadly. "She retired at 67, but then her husband got very sick, cancer. The bills ate through their savings fast. What little was left... it just wasn't enough. And Social Security doesn't cover as much as people think." She took a slow sip of coffee. "So, she took a job. About twenty hours a week, working the morning shift as a greeter and helper at Home Depot."

I pictured sweet, gray-haired Rosa in the orange apron and my heart sank. "Oh no... On her feet all day like that? That's so hard."

Mom nodded. "You've probably seen her, if you ever go to the Home Depot near my house. She's usually in the garden section, helping people carry plants and soil. It's tough on her knees, but she told me she doesn't have a choice. They still have medical debt to pay off and rent and everything."

"That's so unfair," I muttered, feeling anger and sadness churn together. Rosa and her husband were good people. They'd worked hard, they should have been enjoying their grandchildren and having restful mornings, not clocking in at a store.

Mom's eyes welled up, and she stirred her coffee slowly. "Rosa told me the hardest part isn't even the work itself, she's always been a hard worker, you know. It's... it's the way some people look at her. Customers, even coworkers sometimes. Like, 'Oh, poor old lady, she must have messed up to be working at her age.' She said it's like they're judging her, thinking she did something wrong with her life. But she didn't! She and her husband did everything they thought was right. Life just... got so expensive."

I reached across the table and took my mom's hand. I could see the worry in her face, she wasn't just sad for Rosa; she was scared for herself, for all of us.

We sat quietly for a moment. The story of Rosa hit me hard. Retirement felt a long way off for me, I was only in my twenties, but it suddenly felt like something I needed to think about now, not later. Rosa and her husband hadn't planned on getting sick, on losing their savings. Nobody does. That could be my mom in a few years, I realized with a chill. That could even be me, decades down the line, if I didn't start preparing.

"Thank you for telling me," I said softly. "And... don't worry, Mom. I'm going to keep on top of this money stuff. I don't want you or me..." I trailed off, not really wanting to say "ending up in an orange apron at 68," but Mom seemed to read my mind.

She squeezed my hand. "Just promise me you'll save a little when you can, and plan ahead, okay? I never had much to put aside, but I wish I had started sooner. I don't want you to struggle like that."

"I promise," I said, and I meant it. "We're going to be okay."

That night, I lay in my childhood bed thinking about Rosa and my mom and how easily life can change. Rosa's reality felt like a warning from the future: don't assume you'll have time later to save, do it now. I understood, more than ever, why I was fighting so hard to get my finances in order. It wasn't just to get through the month or afford a few treats, it was to build a safety net for the years ahead, for the unexpected, for the day I'd want to retire and not have to pick up a job at an age when I should be resting.

Rosa's story was going to stay with me, pushing me whenever I felt lazy about my budget or tempted to splurge. It was a stark reminder of the importance of planning ahead so we wouldn't be stuck working at an old age in an orange vest unless we truly wanted to be.

Chapter 8: Celebrating with Friends

A few days later, I headed back to Austin to ring in the New Year with my friends. I returned with a belly full of home cooking, a heart full of determination, and, thanks to careful planning, no scary post-holiday bank balance.

Back in Austin for New Year's, our friends' potluck gathering was a smash hit. I spent the afternoon of New Year's Eve turning my apartment into a festive party space on a shoestring budget. We didn't spend a dime on new decorations. Sofia lent me a stack of her homemade paper snowflakes, and I taped them up around the living room windows. I dug out a tangled string of multicolored Christmas lights I'd saved from last year and strung them across the ceiling. Ray arrived early with a folding table and a few extra chairs he'd borrowed from his cousin, so we'd have enough seating for everyone. By the time evening rolled around and the gang started arriving, my little apartment was cozy and twinkling, ready for the holiday party we'd all been looking forward to.

And soon enough, the place was filled with the mouthwatering aroma of all the dishes we'd planned. There were platters of Ray's steaming hot tamales and Dante's beautifully roasted turkey breast (he nailed the recipe, to his own proud surprise), and a big bowl of Lisa's ruby-red hibiscus punch taking center stage on the table. Christmas music played from a Bluetooth speaker in the corner, adding a cheerful background to the clinking of dishes and chatter.

Everyone showed up in their thrift-store holiday sweaters, as promised. We'd even made it a contest: ugliest sweater under $5. The competition was fierce in the most hilarious way. Sofia had found one with a lopsided Christmas tree knitted across the front and proudly sported a blinking light-up necklace to match. I wore an overly festive sweater vest covered in jingly bells that Kayla had dug out of her mom's closet. But Kevin won the prize hands-down when he walked in wearing what can only be described as Rudolph's revenge: a truly hideous green sweater featuring a cross-eyed reindeer with a giant pom-pom for a nose. It was so atrocious that we unanimously voted it the ugliest, and Kevin bowed with a flourish as we applauded his $4 Goodwill masterpiece.

Marisol was thrilled to be part of the celebration. We set up a special "kids' corner" for her in one part of the living room, with a little table just her height. I'd printed out some free holiday coloring pages I found online, and Kevin had even drawn a couple of custom cartoon snowmen and reindeer for her to color in. His art minor skills truly came in handy – Marisol giggled as he sketched a goofy elf with exaggerated ears just for her. Throughout the evening, he sat with her off and on, helping her stay entertained. It warmed my heart to see how our group made sure even the youngest member felt included.

When it was time for gifts, we gathered around my tiny Christmas tree (which Sofia had helped me trim with a few old ornaments and candy canes). Marisol went first, since four-year-olds aren't known for patience. Lisa presented her with the refurbished dollhouse from "Santa" and the little bundle of tablet accessories I had contributed, all wrapped up in a big box. We all held our breath for a second as Marisol tore into the wrapping paper. She let out a squeal of delight at the dollhouse – it was painted bright purple with glittery stars, and you could tell Lisa had poured a lot of love into fixing it up. Then Marisol noticed the sparkly pink tablet case and the sticker packs and other goodies. Her eyes went wide.

"Santa left you a note, Marisol!" Sofia said, handing her an envelope decorated with North Pole stickers. In her best "magical Santa" voice, Sofia read out the letter (which she had penned in looping calligraphy): Santa praised Marisol for being such a good girl and explained that these fun accessories were for the tablet she would get when she was a little older. Marisol listened intently, hugging the tablet case to her chest. By the end of the letter, she was beaming.

"I'm gonna put stickers on the dollhouse *and* save some for my tablet later!" she announced. We all broke into applause and laughter. Lisa caught my eye, and I saw she had tears – the happy kind – shimmering as she smiled. I knew exactly what that meant: relief and joy. Marisol was having a magical Christmas, and no one went into debt to make it happen.

Next it was the grown-ups' turn for our Secret Santa exchange, which turned out to be equal parts heartwarming and hilarious.

I was the lucky one who got to open a gift from Lisa. Inside the small box I found a handmade coupon book tied with a red ribbon. The cover read "For Maya: Because you deserve a break!" I flipped through the pages, and my eyes immediately misted over. Each coupon was handwritten: "Good for one girls' night in with wine and movies – on me," said one. "Good for one free home-cooked meal, delivered to your door," said another in Lisa's neat printing. There was even a coupon for "One pep talk on a bad day – redeemable by phone or in person, any time." I burst out laughing and "awww"ing at the same time. It was so thoughtful and so very Lisa. I got up and gave her a huge hug. "You better believe

I'm redeeming every one of these," I said, sniffing back happy tears.

Across the room, Dante was unwrapping his present from Ray. We all leaned in curiously, because Ray had been very secretive about what he'd found. Dante pulled back the paper and held up an old, collectible comic book. The cover was brightly colored and featured a superhero in a cape lecturing a group of kids about saving money. The title? *Finance Fury* – a vintage comic about financial literacy saving the day. Dante's jaw dropped. "No way! I used to read this as a kid at the library!" he exclaimed. None of us had even known such a comic existed, but trust Ray to dig up something so perfectly tailored. Dante handled the comic like it was gold. "This is amazing, man. Thank you," he said, giving Ray a one-armed hug (while his other hand was already flipping carefully through the yellowed pages).

On the couch, Sofia was opening a gift from Kevin. Kevin looked a bit nervous, fiddling with a loose thread on his sleeve as she did. Inside Sofia's gift bag was a thick binder. The cover had a cute homemade design that said, "Savings for the Stomach and Wallet." Sofia's eyes widened. "What is this?" she murmured, unzipping the binder. As she flipped through, she realized what it was – a collection of recipes. Each plastic-sleeved page had a recipe printout inside, complete with notes. Kevin had compiled cheap, healthy recipes from all over the internet – and added personal touches like little star stickers next to the ones he said he'd already test-cooked himself. He'd even organized it by category: "Easy Weeknight Dinners," "Cheap and Freezable Meals," "Treats on a Budget," and so on. Sofia looked up at him, speechless for a moment, then laughed in delight. "Kevin, did you…make me a cookbook?" she asked. He nodded bashfully. "I know you're always looking for new ideas for your students and yourself, and these are all budget-friendly… I figured, why not collect them?" Sofia launched off her chair to hug him. "This is fantastic! I'm going to try one of these next week," she promised, already flipping back to a page for lentil stew that looked interesting.

When it came time for Kevin to open his present, I found myself suddenly a bit nervous. I was his Secret Santa, and I'd put together the "starter finance kit" I'd imagined. He ripped away the wrapping paper to reveal a sleek leather journal with a note I'd taped to the front: *Kevin's Big Ideas – Funded by Smart Money Moves.* He laughed, opening the cover. Inside, I had written a short message encouraging him to jot down any business ideas or budget plans in that notebook. I'd also tucked a goofy-looking piggy bank shaped like the Texas Capitol dome into the gift bag, wrapped in tissue paper. "So you can save up for your own Capitol one day," I joked. Kevin held up the piggy bank and gave it a little shake, grinning ear to ear. "I love it. And I actually have some ideas that need writing down," he added, waving the journal. We all knew Kevin was destined for big things; maybe this would be the book where he outlined his first startup or something. The thought made him smile even wider.

Ray went next. He tore into a gift bag that had Sofia's name scrawled on the tag. Out from the tissue paper, he pulled a cozy-looking knitted navy-blue beanie and a matching scarf. Sofia, our resident craft queen, had clearly been busy. "I remembered you complaining about the cold on your early shifts at the warehouse," she said with a grin. "I had some leftover yarn in my favorite color, so… surprise!" Ray's face lit up like a kid. He immediately pulled the beanie over his head, it fit like a glove, and wrapped the scarf dramatically around his neck. "How do I look?" he asked, striking a pose. "Muy guapo," Sofia laughed. Ray pretended to strut, then broke into a big grateful smile and went to give Sofia a side hug. "Seriously, thank you. Now I've got no excuse to skip my morning runs, even if it's freezing."

Finally, it was Lisa's turn. She blushed as she opened a neatly wrapped box from Dante. We were all curious, because Dante had been dropping hints that his gift might make a certain little someone very happy. Under the wrapping, Lisa found a gently used board game: the classic Candy Land. She gasped and covered her mouth. "Oh my gosh, we used to play this all the time when I was little!" Sure enough, the Candy Land box looked vintage but in good shape. Dante rubbed the back of his neck, a bit shyly. "You mentioned once how you loved Candy Land as a kid, so when I saw it at the thrift store, I had to grab it. I checked to make sure all the pieces were there and everything. Now you and Marisol can play it together." Lisa looked from Dante to the game, and then unexpectedly she burst into tears – the kind that come when you're completely touched. She threw her arms around Dante. "Thank you," she whispered. "This means so much." Dante patted her back, looking relieved that she liked it. Marisol, hearing the commotion, ran over and squealed, "Candy Land! I play that at my friend's house!" Lisa laughed, wiping her tears quickly so her daughter wouldn't worry, and showed her the box. "Now we have our own, sweetie." The little girl did a happy dance, which made everyone laugh again.

None of our Secret Santa gifts had cost more than a few dollars, but you wouldn't know it from the smiles and excitement in the room. Each gift was so thoughtful and personal that it felt like we'd each spent a million bucks on each other. We were all a little giddy that our experiment in frugality had turned into such a genuinely good time. We laughed until our sides hurt, helped ourselves to second (and third) helpings of dessert, and eventually sprawled out on the couches and floor amid wrapping paper scraps and paper plates, talking about our hopes for the coming year.

Instead of typical New Year's resolutions like "go to the gym" or "get a raise," we found ourselves sharing financially focused goals with each other, because that's where our minds were, and it felt great. We went around the room, each of us offering up a goal.

Sofia kicked it off. "Alright, you guys probably know mine: I'm going to pay off the last $1,000 on my Visa card by March." We all clapped; she was so close to clearing that debt for good.

I chimed in next: "I want to finish saving my emergency fund. Just $500 more to go to hit $3,000. If I'm really strict with myself, I think I can do it by February." My emergency fund had been growing slowly but steadily, and everyone knew how obsessed I was with hitting that milestone.

Lisa went next: "Um, this might sound small, but... I want to start a college fund for Marisol." Dante gave her a thumbs up. "That's awesome," he said. Lisa continued, "Even if it's just $10 a month to start. I figure by the time she's grown, it'll amount to something. And it's more than I had set aside yesterday." We all nodded in encouragement, every journey starts somewhere.

Dante cleared his throat and grinned. "Mine is to increase my 401(k) contribution to 10%. I got a modest year-end bonus at work, and rather than blowing it, I'm going to funnel it straight into investments and up my monthly contribution." "Look at you, planning for retirement already," I teased, but I was impressed. Dante was in his mid-twenties like me, but he was already thinking long-term; after hearing about Rosa, I silently thought that was probably a very good idea.

Ray was next. "I've got about $1,000 left on my credit card balance," he said. "I'm gonna hustle and wipe that out by next December. Pick up a few extra drywall jobs whenever possible... I think I can do it." We all whooped and promised to refer him to anyone we knew who needed home repairs.

Finally, Kevin, who would be graduating in the spring, said, "My goal is to finish school and land a job without any credit card debt tagging along. I have a little balance now, but I'm determined to pay it off and cut it out. Start my post-college life with a clean slate." "Hear, hear!" Dante raised his punch cup toward Kevin. A clean slate – that sounded wonderful.

In my head I was thinking how proud Jim would be. He had emphasized how any goals must be a smart goal if we were going to have a chance to achieve it. I recall what he wrote on his whiteboard at one of our sessions:

SMART Goals

Specific

Measurable

Attainable

Realistic

Time-bound

His teachings had really sunk in with our group and we were now doing this automatically!

After we each shared our goals, we took a moment to appreciate how far we'd come. Kevin stretched his legs out under the coffee table and said, "You guys know what? This is one of the best holiday seasons I've ever had. And guess what, I didn't have to put *any* of it on a credit card."

Sofia raised her glass. "Same here. No holiday debt hangover for once!"

Lisa nodded, her face relaxed and happy. "I was so worried at first, but tonight I feel so grateful. Marisol had an amazing Christmas, and I didn't have to go into debt to make it happen. That's a first for me."

Dante leaned back against the sofa, looking around at all of us. "We actually did it," he said, a satisfied grin spreading across his face. "We had all the holiday fun and none of the financial regret. I'm proud of us, guys."

We clinked our cups of sparkling punch together at that, a little proud circle of budgeteers celebrating our debt-free holiday accomplishment.

As the clock neared midnight on New Year's Eve, we turned the music up and got ready for the countdown. There was no overpriced bar, no DJ, no fancy light show, just us in my living room, a bunch of close friends in goofy sweaters, with sparkling apple cider in our plastic cups and Marisol perched on Lisa's hip, giggling at all the grown-ups getting excited. We turned on the TV just for the final ten seconds of the countdown in Times Square, adding its beeps and flashing numbers to our own chant of "Ten, nine, eight..."

When we got to "Happy New Year!" we all shouted it at the top of our lungs. Dante and Ray uncorked a bottle of cider with a loud pop, and we proceeded to make a mess of my living room with those cheap party poppers that shoot out confetti. Marisol squealed in delight as colorful paper ribbons rained down on us. The rest of us whooped and hugged whoever was closest. The whole room was filled with laughter, the kind that bubbles up and doesn't stop. Outside, distant fireworks crackled across the Austin sky, but I was almost too busy hugging everyone to notice.

I looked around at my friends – truly my extended family – and felt an overwhelming swell of contentment and joy. In that moment, I knew in my heart that this was what the holidays were really about. Not expensive gifts, not trying to impress anyone, but these simple moments of love, gratitude, and hope for the future. We had set out to enjoy the season without spending a fortune, and we'd done it. We proved to ourselves that we could celebrate in style – our own style – without going into debt or feeling deprived. In fact, I honestly couldn't remember a better holiday season than this one, precisely because it was so simple and genuine.

We had weathered the annual onslaught of "spend, spend, spend" by leaning on each other and sticking to what truly mattered. And as we ushered in the new year together, I think we all sensed that 2025 was going to be a good one for us – not without challenges, of course, but we were entering it prepared and united.

If I could handle the temptations of Christmas and the emotional tug of wanting to splurge on my loved ones, then I felt ready for whatever financial tests might come next. Little did I know, my resolve would indeed be tested soon enough, but the foundation we'd built this holiday season was solid.

For now, we clinked our cider glasses once more and made our toasts.

"To a prosperous New Year – for real this time!" Dante declared, raising his cup high.

"¡Próspero Año Nuevo!" Ray added in Spanish, his grin as bright as the fireworks popping outside.

I held up my own cup and echoed, "To prosperity and friendship!"

Our voices and laughter filled the apartment, mixing with the distant booms of fireworks and the pop of another confetti popper Marisol set off. I had never felt richer in spirit than I did right then. As I looked at the beaming faces around me – these friends who had become family – I silently thanked every twist and turn that had led me here. We were ending the year not just better off financially than we started, but better people – more mindful, compassionate, and hopeful about the future. If that wasn't a holiday miracle of our own making, I didn't know what was.

Chapter 9: Reflections

Easter weekend found me driving down I-35 to San Antonio once again, but this time with a lighter heart and a heavier wallet – heavier in the metaphorical sense that for once, I had some breathing room financially. Spring wildflowers dotted the sides of the highway, bluebonnets and Indian paintbrushes painting the landscape in vibrant colors. I rolled down my window to let the warm breeze in, feeling optimistic.

Mom had been dying to have me home for a visit outside the hectic holidays, so I planned a surprise: I'd arrive in time to take her out for a nice lunch and an afternoon on the River Walk, just the two of us. She rarely splurged on such things, always fretting about money. But I'd budgeted for this mini getaway and wanted to treat her.

When I pulled up to our little old house on the south side of San Antonio, Mom came running out, apron on (of course she'd been cooking, despite my telling her I'd bring food). I barely got out of the car before she engulfed me in a hug, squeezing the breath out of me like moms do.

"Mija! You look so good, city life is treating you right," she exclaimed, holding me at arm's length to examine me. "That sweater is nice – new?"

"New to me, thrift store find," I grinned. It was a high-quality brand wool cardigan I'd nabbed for a few bucks. Early on, I'd shared with Mom my thrifting adventures, and now it was like a sport for her too. She proudly told her friends how her daughter learned to dress stylishly on a budget.

Inside, I greeted my *tía* (aunt) who was visiting and my *abuela* (grandma), who now lived with Mom. The house was filled with chatter and a telenovela on TV in the background. After catching up and assuring them that yes, I was eating enough, and no, I wasn't dating anyone serious yet (cue the exaggerated disappointment from Abuela), I told Mom I was kidnapping her for the afternoon.

"Ay, pero – I was making enchiladas," she protested, gesturing to the kitchen.

"They'll keep till dinner. I want to take you out, just us girls," I insisted. "My treat."

She looked like she might argue, but then she broke into a smile and agreed to let my aunt take over kitchen duties. I think she saw the excitement in my eyes and didn't want to dampen it.

We spent the afternoon like tourists in our own hometown. I bought us tickets for the River Walk boat tour – something neither of us had done since I was a kid. As we floated down the river, passing under stone bridges and by cafés with colorful umbrellas, Mom held my hand and pointed out sights as if I hadn't seen them a dozen times. Her delight was infectious; seeing her relaxed and enjoying herself was worth every penny.

Over lunch at a quaint Mexican restaurant by the water, I finally broached the subject I'd been contemplating: Mom's financial situation. Thanks to our earlier budgeting session, I knew she had no savings to speak of and was likely going to work until she physically couldn't. She was only in her early 50s, but years of factory work had taken a toll on her knees and back. And just a few months ago, a round of layoffs at her warehouse had everyone on edge. She thankfully kept her job, but it was a stark reminder of how precarious her situation was. The thought of her suddenly being without a paycheck or a plan made my stomach clench.

"Mama, have you thought about what's next?" I asked gently after we'd savored our tacos al pastor. "Like, how long do you want to keep working at the warehouse?"

She shrugged, eyes dropping to her glass of horchata. "Till I can't, I guess. You know I didn't finish college, and the pay... it's not great, but it's something. Why?"

I took a deep breath, mustering courage. "I've been getting my finances in order, and it's going well. I have a good job now, and I'm saving. I want to help you more, if you'll let me. Not that you can't take care of yourself!" I hurried to add, not wanting to offend her pride. "But you sacrificed so much to put me through school. I want you to be able to rest a bit, maybe work part-time or pursue something you enjoy, not just grind away."

She looked at me with a mix of pride and concern. "Maya, you don't owe me anything. That was my duty as your mother, and I'd do it all again. I don't want to burden you now that you're just starting to build your life."

"It's not a burden. I see it as paying forward what you gave me." I reached across the table to squeeze her hand. "Remember how you always said, 'When you succeed, you pull others up with you'? Well, I *am* succeeding now. And that means I can pull you up a little. I was thinking... maybe you could move to Austin eventually. Not immediately, but perhaps in a year or two. There's work there too, but I'd love to have you close. Maybe I could support you working part-time instead of full-time. We could even take classes together at the community college for fun – you always wanted to learn more about computers, right?"

She laughed, "Ay mija, I'm too old to be in school!" But I could tell the idea warmed her.

"You're never too old. You taught me that learning is lifelong. Look at my friend Lisa – she's in her mid-thirties and back in school to become a dental hygienist. You remember her from the Christmas pictures? The one with the little girl. She's doing it, and she'll nearly triple her income when she finishes. It's inspiring."

Mom shook her head in wonder. "Your friends sound wonderful. I'm so happy you have them. And... maybe I will consider moving up there. My *comadre* (best friend) lives in Round Rock, you know. It would be nice to be near her, and you, of course." She smiled, then added, "But I have to save some money first. Can't show up empty-handed."

"We'll save together," I said firmly. "I'm setting aside a bit each month specifically for you. Think of it as our future 'Mom Fund' – whether it's to help you move or to give you a cushion if you cut down on work. And if you stay here, maybe it's to get your roof fixed or something. Either way, it's happening, so don't try to talk me out of it."

She squeezed my hand, her eyes shiny. "Thank you, Maya. I... I never wanted to lean on you. I wanted you to fly."

"And because of you, I *am* flying. Now it's my turn to be the wind beneath your wings," I quipped, earning an eye-roll for the cheesy line. But a tear escaped her eye even as she laughed.

That evening, as I drove back to Austin, I reflected on how our roles were slowly shifting. Mom would always be my rock, but now I could be hers too. Helping family was a big part of why I wanted to be financially secure, and it fueled my determination to stick to the prosperity path.

Back in Austin, life moved along at a pleasant clip. Meanwhile, big changes were afoot for some of my friends too. Just a few weeks after my San Antonio visit, Ray called me with exciting news: he was under contract to buy his first home. He'd been thinking about homeownership for a while, and now it was finally happening. Ray invited me to tag along for the home inspection that weekend , he said he could use an extra set of eyes and some moral support.

That Saturday morning, I met him at a modest three-bedroom house in Manor, a small town on the outskirts of Austin where prices were more affordable. The home inspector was already there, clipboard in hand. We trailed behind him as he began examining everything from the foundation to the roof.

I could see the excitement in Ray's face as we walked through each empty room. He pointed out the fenced backyard through the kitchen window. "The kids are already planning where to put a swing set," he said with a grin. "They've never had more than a tiny apartment balcony to play on, so this yard is like a dream for them." Inside, he showed me the bedrooms. "My son wants his room painted UT Longhorns orange," Ray chuckled, "and my daughter has decided on purple for hers. They've been sharing a room for years; they're thrilled to each get their own space."

I smiled, picturing his two kids running around here. "I still can't believe you're buying a house," I said, trailing my fingers along the hallway wall. "What made you finally take the plunge? You used to be on the fence about renting versus owning."

Ray leaned against a doorframe, considering. "Yeah, I went back and forth for a long time. Renting was simpler – no huge debt, and if something broke, I just called the landlord. But the rent kept creeping up every year with nothing to show for it. I got tired of that. And with the kids getting older, I wanted more stability for them, you know? A place we can truly call home. I figured if I can swing it, why not put that money toward something of our own instead of paying someone else's mortgage?"

"That makes sense." I nodded, glancing into what would be his kids' bathroom as the inspector ran the faucet. "But owning comes with a lot of expenses too. How did you figure out if you could afford all this?"

"Oh, I ran all the numbers," he replied quickly. "Had to, really. I budgeted out what my monthly mortgage would be *including* homeowners insurance and property taxes. The bank will bundle those into my mortgage payment, so I'll be paying them monthly. It definitely is more responsibility than renting. If something breaks, it's on me now – no more calling the landlord to fix a leaky sink. I've started a 'home maintenance' savings for repairs and upkeep, because things will come up. But even with all that, the monthly payment on this place will be only a couple hundred more than my last rent. And instead of that money vanishing into someone else's pocket, I'll be building equity for my family."

"I'm so impressed," I said, and meant it. "Did our workshop lessons help when you went for the loan? I hear the mortgage process can be pretty intense."

"Big time. The first thing I did was get pre-approved for a mortgage," Ray explained. "The lender went through my finances with a fine-tooth comb. They checked my credit score – thank goodness I knocked out my credit card debt – and they calculated my debt-to-income ratio."

"Debt-to-income... that's DTI, right? I remember hearing about that," I said, recalling the term from one of our workshop sessions.

"Right," he confirmed. "DTI basically means what percentage of your monthly income goes toward debt payments. The bank added up all my monthly debts – my truck loan, credit card minimums, child support, everything – plus what the projected mortgage payment would be. Then they compared that total to my monthly income. They wanted to see a my DTI below 43% to feel confident I could handle the mortgage on top of everything else. I've kept mine a lot lower than that, around the low 30s, which worked in my favor. If I was still drowning in debt, I might not have qualified at all."

I remembered how not long ago Ray had worried about making even minimum payments. Now he was casually talking about mortgage criteria and percentages like a pro. I couldn't help but smile.

"So once you got pre-approved, you started house hunting?" I prompted.

"Yep. Knowing my budget from the pre-approval, I got a realtor to help me look at places in that price range. My realtor, Liz Montoya, is great: super knowledgeable, helpful, and really explains things so I, as a first-time home buyer, can understand. As a buyer, having an agent didn't cost me anything out of pocket – the seller covers the commission – and she's been awesome.

She found this place and helped me make a strong offer. When the seller accepted, we had a 7-day *option* period, during which we could back out if anything negative presented itself. Our option period ends tomorrow so that's why we had to get the inspection today so that we had a day to negotiate any necessary repairs or credits. I hope the inspector doesn't find anything wrong with the place that we have to address with the seller!

The contract also includes *earnest money*, typically 1% of the purchase price. I had to write a check to the title company for this, along with my check for a small option fee, after signing. The earnest money only activates once we pass through the option period, after which it *goes hard,* as these real estate people like to say. This means that if I change my mind, for no good reason, before closing, the seller gets the money.

We will then enter the escrow phase to take care of all the due diligence." He waved a hand as the inspector climbed a ladder into the attic. "Like today: the inspection. Next comes the appraisal the bank does to make sure the house is worth the price. If all that checks out, I'll sign the final papers and get the keys in probably 3-4 weeks."

"How much did you have to put down for the house?" I asked, curious. "I always hear you need 20% or something crazy."

Ray chuckled. "If I'd needed 20%, I wouldn't be here! For first-time buyers there are options. I'm actually using an FHA loan – that's a government-backed loan – so I only need to put down 3.5% of the purchase price. And I qualified for a state first-time homebuyer program that helped with a chunk of my down payment. I took a homebuyer education class they offered – learned a ton, by the way – and in return I got a few thousand dollars as a grant. Between that and what I've been saving these past couple years, I scraped together enough for the down payment *and* the closing costs."

"Closing costs – that's another thing I wouldn't have thought of a year ago," I said, shaking my head. We'd learned about them in theory, but here was Ray actually paying them. "Those are like the fees and stuff, right?"

"Yeah, all the extra fees you pay at the end to actually close the deal," he said. "Things like the appraisal fee, title insurance, lender fees, home insurance for the first year, property tax escrow – it adds up to several thousand dollars. Usually around 3 to 5% of the purchase price in total. I managed to negotiate for the seller to cover a part of it – but I'm still on the hook for a good chunk. My agent really helped with these and other negotiations and got me a better deal than I could have on my own, this being my first deal. Thanks Liz! I'm glad I planned for this purchase well in advance. Honestly, if we hadn't been budgeting and saving like we have, I wouldn't have been able to pull it off."

I gave him an appreciative grin. "Honestly, seeing you do this makes it feel more reachable for me someday. You make it look easy, but I know it's not."

He smiled back, a little bashfully. "If I can do it, any of us can. I mean that. A year ago I thought owning a home was impossible for someone like me. But I changed my mindset – *you all* helped me change it. Instead of thinking 'that's not for people like us,' I started asking, 'how *can* I make it happen?' And here I am, almost at the finish line." He put his hand on my shoulder. "I can't thank you enough, Maya. You and the gang… y'all kept me going."

Before I could protest that it was all him, the inspector returned to the living room, wiping a bit of attic dust off his hands. He reported a few minor findings – a leaky faucet here, an AC filter that needed replacing there – but no major red flags. Ray let out a breath he'd been holding and broke into a grin.

"Looks like there's nothing that would break the deal," the inspector said, packing up his tools. "Just address these minor issues and you'll be good. I'll email you the full report so you can go over it with your agent."

Ray shook the inspector's hand and promised to follow up on the fixes. After the inspector left, I nudged Ray playfully. "Congratulations, homeowner-to-be!"

He laughed, a mixture of joy and disbelief on his face. "It's really happening."

"I'm so happy for you. Your kids are going to love it here," I said, giving him a side hug. I could already imagine the two little ones racing through the hall.

"They really are," he nodded, eyes bright. "I can't wait to see them playing in that yard. Maybe after I get the keys and do a little cleaning, I'll have you all over for a housewarming potluck. One with *real* furniture," he added with a chuckle, glancing around the empty living room.

"Just say when – we'll all be there, plastic folding chairs and all," I teased. As I headed out to my car, I took one last look at the house – a simple, cozy starter home that was about to become the center of Ray's family life. I felt a swell of pride. Ray's journey from worrying about making rent to buying this home was incredible. It made me even more excited for our next money gang meet-up; I knew we'd have some serious celebrating to do.

Sure enough, a few weeks later at our monthly "accountability dinner," we had plenty to celebrate. We all squeezed into Dante's apartment that evening, balancing paper plates of potluck enchiladas and salad on our laps. When it came time to share updates, I proudly announced that I was officially credit card debt-free. It hadn't been easy. For the past 8 months I'd been working 15 hours a week extra, after my day job, driving Uber in the evenings, and bakery work on the weekends, just to pay this off. It felt great to finally be free. And exhausted.

The group whooped and clapped in unison, and Dante jokingly knighted me with a spatula as the "Queen of No Balances." I played along, bowing graciously. It felt like one of the biggest milestones yet, considering a year ago I'd had thousands in high-interest debt with no plan. My spreadsheet was starting to look healthier.

Net Worth = Assets - Liabilities			
Assets		**Liabilities**	
401(k)	$4,190	Credit Cards	$0
Investments	$1,000	Student Debt	$21,750
Savings	$3,500		
Total	$8,690	Total	$21,750
Net Worth =	**-$13,060**		

After the laughter and cheers died down, our conversation turned to life's curveballs. Not long ago, we would have avoided talking about scary "what if" scenarios, but now it felt safe to acknowledge them. The topic of job security came up – we'd all seen headlines about layoffs in various industries. Instead of collective anxiety, we shared a surprising sense of resilience.

"My and Maya's company actually had a small round of layoffs last month," Dante admitted, pushing up his glasses. "A year ago, that would've had me losing sleep. But this time... I mean, I *worried*, I'm only human. But I also knew we'd be okay even if I was cut. I've got savings to cover 4 months of expenses (so far), no credit card debt hanging over me, and heck – worst case, I could drive Uber for a bit while job hunting." He gave a wry smile and raised his iced tea in a mock toast. "Being financially stable is the best safety net, huh?"

Sofía nodded vigorously. "Same here. The school I work for lost a big grant, and there were rumors of budget cuts. Before, I would've been panicking at the thought of losing my job – I had *zero* savings back then. Now I've got a cushion to fall back on and even a side gig doing graphic design. I know I could bounce back if I had to."

We went around the room and Kevin joined on Face Time, each of us chiming in. Lisa mentioned that if the dental office she worked at didn't need her anymore, she'd pick up some hours at the campus dental clinic while also looking at temporary office jobs. She'd tap her emergency fund if needed. Even Ray – grinning ear to ear over a plate of enchiladas – said that having a house full of kids made him double down on building an emergency fund for whatever surprises might come.

It struck me how much our mindsets had shifted. Life still had its uncertainties, but we no longer felt helpless against them. We had plans and back-ups, and that gave us confidence. Just one year earlier, the mere whisper of "layoff" or "unexpected bill" would have set off panic. Now we talked about these things openly, trading tips on side gigs and backup plans as casually as we once traded happy hour recommendations. We knew how to bend without breaking.

Kevin had graduated from UT and moved to Seattle for his first professional job so couldn't be with us in person. We were all impressed that he wanted to stay in our group even from another city. We passed the phone around so everyone could say hi to him on video. He told us about how he'd chosen an apartment he could afford even on half his new salary, just in case. Life was good up in Washington – his software job was challenging but exciting – and he joked that he missed Texas BBQ almost as much as he missed us. We made him promise to visit soon (and to bring back some rain, since Seattle had plenty to spare).

Sofía shared that she had recently moved into her very own rented duplex unit. Money was tight on her teacher salary, but she was managing it carefully. We even helped her paint the living room a sunny yellow one weekend, doing a DIY décor uplift on a budget. Sofía beamed as she described having her own space. It was small and a bit old, but it was *hers*. "Worth every penny," she said, clinking her soda can to toast to independence.

Dante had an exciting update too: he'd put in for an internal promotion at his company – something he admitted he wouldn't have had the confidence to do before getting his finances under control. "I always thought I needed to job-hop to get ahead," he said, "but it turns out I might be able to move up right where I am. Worst they can say is no, right?" (Those were his words a month ago when he applied.) Spoiler: they didn't say no. By late summer he was promoted to team lead, complete with a pay bump that he immediately directed toward maxing out his Roth IRA. We teased him that he was turning into *that guy* who immediately invests his raise, but we were all proud.

Lisa was deep into her dental hygiene program and absolutely thriving. It wasn't easy – juggling her full time job, classes, clinic hours, and raising her daughter – but the glow on her face whenever we asked about school said it all. She was on track to finish near the top of her class, and none of us doubted she'd do it. She'd even started hosting weekend study groups at her apartment for a few classmates, complete with coffee and homemade snacks. "They ask me how I keep it all together," she recounted, laughing, "and I say: lots of help and a *budget*!" At this, we all raised our glasses because we knew exactly what she meant. Her younger classmates now saw her as a bit of a "mom" figure, and she'd passed along many of the workshop tips we taught her – spreading the wisdom, one study session at a time.

Ray, now a proud homeowner, was probably the busiest of all of us. By our mid-summer dinner he had closed on his house and spent any spare moment on DIY projects to make it a home. He joked that owning a house was like taking on a part-time job – his weekends had turned into a blur of painting walls, fixing leaky faucets, and mowing his very own lawn. "It's a labor of love," he said with a grin. Despite his packed schedule, he still carved out time to help Jim set up workshops or give testimonials (as we all did now and then). And in true Ray fashion, he had roped his kids into a little entrepreneurial venture: they were building and selling handmade birdhouses to raise money for their college funds – an idea sparked after Ray taught them about saving and compound interest. "They've sold ten so far, can you believe it?" he told us proudly. "Little entrepreneurs! I promised I'll match whatever they make and put it in their accounts." Seeing how our changes were trickling down to the next generation was incredibly rewarding.

By the time fall rolled around, I found myself reflecting on the dramatic turn my life had taken since that fateful night at the grocery store. I visited that same H-E-B recently and smiled at the memory – it felt like looking at a different person in a different lifetime. This time, I filled my cart with groceries I'd budgeted carefully for, used my coupons and the store app for deals, and paid with my debit card confidently, knowing exactly how much was in my account (and that there was a comfortable buffer). No heart palpitations, no shame. I realized I wasn't even afraid of the "what ifs" that used to haunt me – what if a surprise expense popped up, or what if I lost my job one day – because I'd built a safety net. I knew I could handle the unexpected and bounce back from any setback. That peace of mind was worth as much as the money in the bank.

In fact, I even struck up a lighthearted conversation with the cashier about the price of avocados, of all things. As I walked out, bags in hand, I actually felt... *happy*. That grocery store – once the scene of my humiliation – had become just a regular stop in my week, maybe even a pleasant one when I planned it right.

To celebrate how far we all had come, our group decided to throw a "Prosperity Party" in mid-October – basically an excuse to enjoy ourselves and toast our achievements together. The timing was perfect: not only did it mark a year since our original workshop graduation, but Kevin was flying back to town for a visit. (His Seattle job gave him a week off, and he insisted his main reason for coming was to see us – though a craving for Texas BBQ was a close second, he joked.)

The party wasn't lavish, of course – in true frugal style, we rented a pavilion at Zilker Park for a few bucks and had an outdoor picnic, potluck-style. But I did splurge on one special treat as a surprise: I ordered a big custom cake from Lisa, iced with the words "Congrats, Financial Freedom Fighters!" and little frosting figures representing each of us. Lisa wanted to do it for free but I wouldn't allow it. I told her I'd been saving up for this for like 2 months, so reluctantly she accepted. I know she put way more time into our cake than any other, and the results were amazing.

When I unveiled the cake at the party, everyone doubled over laughing at the tiny frosting versions of Dante's glasses and Lisa's scrubs and Ray's toolbelt. We took about a thousand pictures. It felt amazing to be able to do something like that for my friends without worrying that I was breaking my budget.

As the sun set over the Austin skyline that evening at Zilker, painting the sky in oranges and purples, I sat on a picnic blanket and soaked it all in. Ray strummed a guitar softly (turns out he played a little in his youth) while Kevin and a friend's energetic dog chased a frisbee. Lisa was gently swaying to the music, eyes closed, probably daydreaming about her graduation day. Dante was animatedly explaining some stock market concept to Sofía, who was nodding politely until she could get a word in to teasingly tell him that he'd become the boring finance lecturer we used to fear Jim might be. ("Hey, I'll gladly lecture if it means everyone retires a millionaire!" Dante shot back, which made all of us laugh.)

I leaned back on my elbows and let out a contented sigh. *This* was wealth, right here – not the kind in bank accounts (though those were improving too), but the kind in heart, in friendship, in community.

With the first stars starting to peep out and the sound of laughter and guitar chords in the air, I thought about what Mom had said back in San Antonio: she wanted me to fly. In that moment I realized I wasn't just flying solo anymore; I had a whole flock. We all were flying, lifting each other higher as we rose.

In a quiet moment, I snapped a mental picture of the scene – my dear friends gathered together, the city we called home glowing in the background, and the feeling of limitless possibility mixed with the warm security of knowing we were prepared for whatever might come.

Tomorrow, we'd all go back to our routines – work, classes, family duties – but we would do so armed with the knowledge that we had changed our lives for the better, one step at a time.

Little did I know, we were about to come full circle with an opportunity to share our journey on a bigger stage – a chance to truly pay it forward, just as I'd been doing with Mom and as we had been doing with the workshop groups. But as with everything in this journey, when the time came, we'd embrace it together.

Chapter 10: Setback and Support

Just when it seemed like things were on an unstoppable upward trajectory, life threw a curveball my way. In early January, right after the holidays, the startup where Dante and I worked announced a major downsizing. I guess the layoffs last year weren't enough. Our biggest client had pulled out and a round of funding fell through. The company leadership tried to be upbeat, but the grim faces in HR said it all.

I remember sitting in a small conference room, a box of tissues on the table (never a good sign), as the HR manager informed me that my position was impacted. Wait, what? Me? It felt surreal. I got all excellent performance reviews and my boss and I got along really well. This must be some sort of mistake! I had seen layoffs happen to others during the pandemic years prior, but now it was happening to me. My chest tightened and my vision blurred at the edges as I fought back tears and the urge to panic.

They handed me a final paycheck, including a modest two-week severance. I managed to ask about my health insurance, covered until the end of the month, then I'd have to figure something out. Numbly, I carried my little box of desk belongings (a couple of notebooks, a plant, a framed photo of Mom and me at graduation) to my car. It was eerily similar to how I'd felt leaving the grocery store that night my card was declined: exposed, uncertain, ashamed. Only this time it wasn't due to something I did; it was beyond my control. Somehow, that made it both easier and harder.

Dante found me in the parking lot. He still had a job, his role in product development was safe, for now, but he looked almost as devastated as I felt. "Maya... I am so sorry," he said softly. "This is so unfair."

I tried to smile bravely. "I'll be okay. At least one of us is still in, right?" But my voice wavered.

He surprised me with a hug, office formalities be damned. "Listen, whatever you need, if I hear of any openings elsewhere, I'll let you know. And you're gonna bounce back, I know it. You've been busting your butt budgeting and saving. You've got that cushion now, right?"

He was right and that thought steadied me. I had about $6,000 in my emergency fund now. I had taken a break from my nighttime rideshare driving but was still able to save $400 a month, in addition to everything else, so that felt really good. Plus I could trim expenses to stretch the severance. I wasn't zeroed out this time, far from it. Not having any high interest credit card debt was a huge relief. I ran my spreadsheet in my head.

Net Worth = Assets - Liabilities			
Assets		**Liabilities**	
401(k)	$4,850	Credit Cards	$0
Investments	$1,000	Student Debt	$20,250
Savings	$5,900		
Total	$11,750	Total	$20,250
Net Worth =	**-$8,500**		

Still, that afternoon, alone in my apartment (Kayla was out), I let myself collapse on the couch and cry hard for a solid half-hour. Losing a job felt personal, even if logic said it wasn't.

Questions swirled: What did I do wrong? How will I find something new in this economy? What if I fail?

After the storm of tears passed, I sat up and grabbed a notebook. I needed a plan, something to focus on to replace the fear. Taking a deep breath, I wrote:

Operation Bounce Back

1. File for unemployment benefits (I remembered reading how that's what it's there for, no shame in using it while you search).
2. Update resume and LinkedIn.
3. Reach out to contacts (former classmates, professors, mentors).
4. Search job boards daily (Indeed, LinkedIn, Glassdoor, company career pages).
5. Budget adjustment: pause extra debt payments, minimize expenses, use emergency fund for essentials as needed.

6. Take care of myself (exercise, eat well, sleep) so I don't burn out or fall into depression during the search.

Listing those out gave me a sense of control. I started on number 1 immediately, spending an hour navigating the Texas Workforce Commission site to file for unemployment insurance. The benefits wouldn't be a lot, maybe enough to cover 50-60% of my take-home pay for a few months, but combined with my emergency fund, I could squeak by.

After hitting "submit" on that application, I opened up the budgeting spreadsheet I'd been maintaining and got to work on task #5: adjusting my finances for lean times. I listed all my fixed costs, rent, utilities, groceries, minimum debt payments, then looked for anything I could trim or pause. The subscription box I'd been meaning to cancel? Gone. My Netflix and music streaming? On hold; I could survive on free entertainment from the library or YouTube for now. Dining out and coffee runs would have to be cut way back too. It was a little painful to remove these small comforts, but I reminded myself it was only temporary. Every dollar I didn't spend on non-essentials was one more dollar I could keep for essentials like rent and gas.

I also accepted that I'd likely have to tap into my emergency fund soon, and that's exactly what it was there for. Instead of feeling guilty or anxious about using that money, I tried to take pride in the fact that I'd prepared for a rainy day. Well, the rain had arrived. Thanks to that cushion, I could keep a roof over my head and food on the table while I searched for a new job.

As dusk fell, Kayla returned from campus and found me hunched over my laptop, surrounded by a notepad, crumpled tissues, and budgeting scribbles. The moment she saw my red, puffy eyes, she knew something was wrong.

"Maya? What's going on?" she asked, concern all over her face as she dropped her backpack and came to my side.

I took a shaky breath. "I... got laid off today," I managed to say quietly. Saying it out loud made it more real, and my eyes welled up again. "The company downsized, and my job was cut."

"Oh no, I'm so sorry," Kayla exclaimed, wrapping her arms around me in a tight hug. I clung to her, grateful for the comfort. After a minute, she pulled back and looked me in the eye. "What do you need? Chocolate? A stiff drink? To vent? Seriously, I'm here for whatever."

I half-laughed through my sniffles. "Maybe just having you here is enough for now. I... I've already started figuring out my next steps," I said, gesturing at my notebook and laptop. "Filed for unemployment, updating my resume next, and... trying not to freak out."

Kayla nodded, her expression both proud and concerned. "That's good. But listen, I mean it: whatever you need. If money gets tight, I can cover more of the groceries for a bit, or the electricity bill, whatever. We'll make it work. I can cut back too or dip into my savings. Don't even worry about that."

I felt a fresh rush of emotion at her offer. "Thank you, but I think I'll be okay for now," I said. "I have a little emergency fund saved up and there's a severance check, so that should carry me for a couple of months at least if I'm careful. But... it means so much to know you've got my back. I promise I'll tell you if it gets bad, okay?"

"Deal," she said softly. "And hey, I'll ask around in my network. Maybe one of my colleagues knows about a job opening or some freelance work you could do. I did hear recently that the campus museum was looking for a social media coordinator. I'll find out more."

I managed a small smile. Trust Kayla to already be brainstorming solutions. "You're the best. Really."

"No, you'd do the same for me," she replied, giving my shoulder a squeeze. "Now, how about I make us some grilled cheese? Comfort food is step one of my crisis management plan."

I let out a watery laugh. "That sounds perfect." As she busied herself in the kitchen, I realized I felt significantly calmer. The situation still sucked, no doubt about it, but I was reminded I wasn't in it alone.

Later that evening, as we sat on the couch with our grilled cheese sandwiches, my phone began buzzing on the coffee table. One message after another lit up the screen. The news of my layoff had spread among my friends, and they were reaching out with love and support:

- Sofia: "Heard about your job. I'm so sorry! You've got this though. Let's do coffee tomorrow? My treat.:))"
- Lisa: "If you need anything at all, I'm here. Even just a vent session. Also, I have some coupons for groceries I won't use; I'll drop them by."
- Kevin: "That sucks! If I hear of any marketing jobs around campus or anything else from my UT contacts, I'll send them your way. Hang in there!"

- Jim: "Maya, Dante told me the news. Very sorry to hear. I do know a couple of folks at UT's communications office and at a nonprofit who might be looking for someone with your skills. Let me know if you'd like me to connect you. And remember, setbacks happen, but you're prepared for this. Call anytime."

Reading those messages, I felt a swell of something unexpected: gratitude. Jim's reminder that I was *prepared* for this setback especially resonated, helping to chase away the last shadows of panic. Just months ago, I'd have hidden in shame with a crisis like this. Now, I had an army of supporters cheering me on. It made me believe that losing this job might just be a setback, not the end of the world.

Later that night, my phone rang. It was Kevin calling. I picked up, and his warm, slightly nervous voice came through.

"Hey Maya, how are you holding up?" he asked gently.

"I'm... doing okay, all things considered," I said. "It was rough at first, not gonna lie. But I'm feeling better now that I've had time to process a bit."

"I was really worried about you," Kevin admitted. "Getting laid off can really mess with your head. I remember when my dad got laid off a few years back, our whole family was stressed. So I kind of get it, at least secondhand."

"Thanks. Yeah, it's been a rollercoaster of a day," I sighed. "I went from shock, to ugly crying, to action mode writing up a job-hunt plan."

Kevin chuckled softly. "That sounds like you, once a planner, always a planner. Speaking of, have you figured out, like, your financial situation for the next little while? Not to pry, but you taught me all about budgeting, so I'm just checking..."

"It's okay, I appreciate it," I assured him. "I actually sat down and crunched the numbers earlier. First off, I got 2 weeks severance so that give me an early cushion. Then unemployment benefits cover a portion of my monthly critical expenses and can extend up to 6 months, so that's a nice additional comfort. I'm still putting in like 5 hours a week for the bakery, so that an ongoing $500 or so a month. And then I've got close to 3 months of critical expenses saved in my emergency fund so I think I'll be alright for up to 6 months if I'm really frugal."

"That's a relief," he said, sounding genuinely happy. "I mean, it still sucks you lost your job, but hearing that you can cover a few months takes a lot of pressure off, right? Like, you won't have to grab the first sketchy gig that comes along just to pay rent next month."

"Exactly. Knowing I have a bit of a runway really calms me down," I agreed. "Honestly, I wouldn't have had any cushion a year ago. I would've been panicking about rent and probably maxing out my credit card by tomorrow."

"But instead you built that cushion brick by brick," Kevin pointed out. "And now it's doing its job, keeping you safe. The power of an emergency fund, huh? You always told us to save for a rainy day... and well, it's raining. But you have an umbrella now."

I laughed quietly. "You're right. It feels really good knowing past me had future me's back. I'm still scared, but it's not the same kind of desperation as before."

"Exactly. And hey, if there's anything I can do to help stretch that budget, you let me know. I could show you my super cheap chili recipe or something," he added, making me smile.

"You, cooking? That I'd pay to see," I teased.

"Very funny," he said. "Seriously though, you got this, Maya. You've worked so hard to turn things around, and I'm honestly so proud of you. I know I haven't known you as long as some of the others, but you've kind of been like an awesome big sister teaching me all this life stuff. So... now it's my turn to remind you of what you taught us: you've got savings, a plan, and a whole team behind you. No panicking, okay?"

I felt a lump in my throat (in a good way). "Okay. No panicking," I promised.

"Good. Keep your head up. Call me anytime, even if you just want to procrastinate by talking about the latest superhero show or something," he said.

I smiled. "I will. Thanks, Kev."

After we hung up, I sat for a moment in the quiet of my living room, absorbing the events of the day. It struck me how much had changed in a year, how I could discuss an "emergency fund" and a multi-month runway with a sense of calm, instead of choking on anxiety. And how incredible my friends were. Kevin, still in college, was giving me a pep talk like a seasoned coach. I went to bed that night feeling, for the first time since the layoff, more hopeful than fearful about the future.

True to her word, Sofia showed up the next morning, Saturday, with two cups of coffee and a box of pastries from a local bakery. We sat at my kitchen table as I polished up my resume and she gave feedback. With her sharp eye (she was an English teacher, after all), she helped me phrase things more powerfully: "Don't say 'assisted with social media campaigns', say 'spearheaded social media campaigns reaching X users.' Own it, girl!"

We also tailored my resume for different kinds of roles, tech marketing, higher ed communications, even non-profit PR. Austin had a variety of industries, and I was open-minded.

That weekend, I sent out my first batch of applications, ten in total. It felt oddly empowering clicking that send button, each one a possible new chapter.

Meanwhile, true to her generous spirit, Lisa swung by Sunday afternoon with an envelope of grocery coupons and a Tupperware of home-cooked enchiladas. "For you and Kayla," she said. "I figured you probably don't feel like cooking. And these are good to freeze if you want to save some for later."

I nearly cried (again) at her kindness. Marisol had drawn a little smiley face in crayon on the container lid, with the words "Feel better Miss Maya." That made me actually laugh. I gave Lisa a hug. "Thank you. This means more than you know."

Monday morning, I dressed as if I were going to work, jeans and a nice blouse, casual but presentable. I set up at my laptop in the living room and treated the job search like a 9-to-5. I followed up on applications, wrote cover letters tailored to each position, and did some online courses on LinkedIn Learning to add a few skills to my toolkit (there was one on Google Analytics I'd been meaning to do, now I had time).

Each day, I took a break to jog a couple of miles or do a yoga video, keeping my stress in check. It was tempting to mope or sleep in, but I remembered Jim's advice: treat it like a job and also invest in yourself.

Throughout, Dante checked in with updates from his end. He'd spoken to a friend at Dell who said I could list him as a reference. Sofia's cousin worked at Austin ISD's communications department and was putting in a word for me. As promised, Kayla had put out feelers among her network, and one of them sent me the link for the social media manager position at a local museum.

By the second week, I had a few callbacks and an interview lined up at a mid-sized tech firm. The night before that first interview, I was nervous. It had been a couple of years since I'd interviewed anywhere. Dante and Sofia both offered to do a mock interview with me over Zoom, which was equal parts hilarious and helpful (Dante put on a fake stiff voice, "Tell me about a time you demonstrated leadership," making me and Sofia crack up, but then we actually practiced serious answers).

The interview went well. So did a couple of others that followed, including one at the University of Texas itself for a communications coordinator role. Walking onto the UT campus in professional attire, heading to the Tower for an interview, felt surreal. The last time I'd been in that building was as a student, nervously turning in a final project. Now I was here as an adult, positioning myself as someone who could contribute to the institution.

Maybe it was that familiarity or just the alignment of my background, but I clicked with the team there. They appreciated my tech startup experience and social media savvy, saying the university was looking to modernize its outreach to younger audiences. I left that interview with a good feeling.

The next month was more of the same. I continued to treat my job search like a job, getting dressed every morning and working on resumes, applications, learning new skills, and networking with anyone I could. I grew a lot, had a lot of inspiring conversations, but no job offers. Prepping for each interview was *almost* fun, but then not hearing back afterwards was depressing. It always sounds so positive when we're on the call, but I feel like so often they just say nice things like, "we'll be in touch," or "we think you'd be a great fit for this role," but then they disappear. Anyway… onwards and upwards…

Two months after getting laid off, two offers came in almost back to back: the tech firm and UT Austin. The tech firm offered slightly higher pay; UT offered slightly better benefits (and frankly, a cause I cared about, education). It was decision time.

I consulted my personal board of advisors (a.k.a. the group chat). They helped me weigh pros and cons. I also remembered one of the workshop lessons: salary negotiation. In the past, I'd have just been grateful and said yes immediately. This time, I carefully inquired with each if there was wiggle room. The tech firm was firm on their number but UT actually agreed to a small bump in salary when I asked (turns out they had a range and I was at the lower end; asking moved me up a bit). It wasn't huge, but it meant about $3,000 more a year, nothing to sneeze at.

In the end, I chose the UT Austin job. It felt right to return to my alma mater, to be part of something that had given me so much. Plus, the stability of a large institution and the tuition benefit (I could take some classes for free as staff) were perks that appealed to me; maybe I'd go to grad school part-time down the line with that benefit.

Signing the offer letter, I felt a wave of relief and pride wash over me. In just two months, I'd gone from jobless to landing an even better opportunity. And I managed it without spiraling into financial ruin or existential dread (well, only a little dread on the darkest nights). The safety nets I'd put in place, my emergency savings, supportive friends, improved skills, had worked. In fact, in two months of unemployment, considering my severance pay and state unemployment benefits, I only used $1,500 from my emergency fund!

On my first day at UT, I parked in the staff lot and took a moment to soak it in. I could see the iconic UT Tower against the blue sky. Students bustled past on their way to class, and I felt a kinship with them and with my younger self who'd walked these paths full of dreams. Life had come somewhat full circle, yet I was in such a different place now.

I felt so accomplished when I completed my employment paperwork and elected to contribute 5% of my salary to the university's 401(k) plan, taking full advantage of their matching program. I had already updated my bank settings to automatically divert 10% of my take-home income to my high interest savings account and an extra 5% to my new brokerage account for investing. That's a total of 20% savings – Darren, would be so proud!

That evening, our whole gang met at a casual BBQ spot to celebrate my new job (and because Ray insisted he had a coupon for a platter deal that would feed everyone at a bargain). As we sat at a picnic table eating smoked turkey and brisket, I looked around at these people from all walks of life, an artist-turned-techie (Dante), a teacher (Sofia), a handyman and family man (Ray), a single mom (Lisa), and recent college grad and computer guy (Kevin) who joined by phone again. At one point, I realized: no one was freaking out about money in that moment. Sure, we all still had challenges, Ray was building up a nest egg in order to start his own business, Lisa was juggling work and the cake business, Sofia was planning to move out on her own soon and knew money would be tight, but everyone had a plan and confidence. And we had each other.

It hit me how proud I was of all of us. Not one person at this table would be considered "rich" by society. But we were richer in knowledge and community than many people ever get to be.

"To Maya's new chapter!" Sofia toasted with her sweet tea.

"And to many more successes for all of us," I added, lifting my lemonade. We clinked and drank, the tangy lemonade symbolizing both the sweetness and sourness of recent events, life had given me lemons, indeed, but I'd made something resembling lemonade out of it.

As the evening wound down, Kevin was proud to share that upon starting the new job he immediately chose to max out his 401(k) contributions and get the maximum company match. (I guess we had both learned well.) He also bragged that he had more savings in his bank account than any of his new friends in Washington State. A good brag.

In that moment, I realized how far-reaching our little group's impact was. We weren't just handling our own money better; we were growing in confidence to chase bigger dreams, whether it was further education, new careers, or moving to new places.

As I drove home that night, I reflected on how a setback that could have been devastating turned into a catalyst for growth. Losing my job tested everything I'd learned: having savings, a support network, and the resilience to adapt. In the past, I might have fallen apart. Now, I felt almost grateful it happened, because it proved to me that I could handle life's punches. I slept deeply that night, knowing that whatever the future held, I wouldn't be facing it alone and I'd face it with the hard-won wisdom of the past year.

Chapter 11: Paying It Forward

One year later, on a bright Spring evening, I found myself back at the Carver Library in East Austin, the very place where this journey truly began. Only this time, I wasn't there as a participant, but as a guest speaker.

Jim had kept in touch with all of us, and earlier in the winter he asked if some of us might speak to a new cohort of the Personal Finance Workshop. He wanted the newbies to hear real success stories from people like us, who had sat in those same chairs. We all eagerly agreed.

Now, as I stood outside the meeting room with Sofia and Dante by my side, I felt a flutter of nerves reminiscent of that first night. But it was a good kind of nervous, the kind that comes with gratitude and excitement.

"Can you believe it's been more than 2 years since we finished Jim's program?" Sofia whispered, straightening the name badge they'd given her.

"Nope. Feels like yesterday and a lifetime ago at once," I whispered back.

We peeked in. About a dozen fresh faces were seated in a circle, fidgeting, probably anxious about sharing their money troubles. I recognized that look so well. In the front, Jim caught my eye through the glass door and gave us an encouraging nod.

He introduced us one by one: Sofia, now 31 and recently promoted to head of her department's curriculum team at the high school (she'd modestly told us it's because she learned to manage money so well she could afford the time to take a leadership course, but we knew it was her talent too). Dante, now 29, who had started an MBA program at UT in the evenings and even launched a small tech blog that earned a bit of side income. And me, Maya, 28, representing "what a difference a year can make," as Jim kindly put it. Ray wasn't up front with us just yet; he'd texted that he was running late from a job, but we hoped he'd make it in time. I also spotted Darren quietly slipping into a chair at the back of the room, freshly back in town after months away. Jim had a special plan to have him speak later in the session.

One by one, we shared our stories.
Sofia went first. She described how she used to feel hopeless about money, drowning in student loans and credit card debt, but learned to budget, pay off one of her cards, and even save enough to move into her own small rented cottage (no more roommates). She admitted she still drove her old car and shopped clearance sales, but now it was by choice to meet her bigger goals, like saving for a home in a couple of years. The new attendees looked at her with admiration, especially one young woman in scrubs who likely related to the modest salary struggle.

Dante spoke about lifestyle creep, how when he first got his tech job he spent money as fast as it came on gadgets and going out, assuming the good times would roll forever. The layoff scare at our old startup was a wake-up call; he realized he needed to build an emergency fund and invest in himself. He proudly shared that he now maxes out his 401(k) ("I figured if I don't see it, I don't miss it," he joked, getting laughs) and that he's paying for his MBA course-by-course in cash, thanks to diligent saving and some freelance consulting he did on weekends. A couple of the young guys in the audience nodded, clearly seeing a bit of themselves in him.

Then it was my turn. I took a deep breath, meeting the eyes of a middle-aged man in a work uniform, a college student clutching a notebook, a single mom with a toddler on her lap. "Hi, I'm Maya," I began. "Just over two years ago, I was sitting where you are, feeling overwhelmed. I'd done everything 'right' according to the world, went to college, got the job, yet I was living paycheck to paycheck, stressed and ashamed of my money problems."

I recounted the infamous grocery store incident and saw knowing winces around the room. I told them how the workshop gave me not just knowledge, but a community. How I learned to budget, pay off credit card debt, and build a safety net. And then, when I lost my job, those changes saved me. "Because I had a plan and support, I not only got through unemployment without going into a panic or massive debt, I actually landed on my feet in a better position. I'm now working at UT in communications, a job I love, and I've built back my emergency fund to cover six months of expenses." That last part got a few eyebrows raised, it felt good to be able to say it, knowing how impossible that once sounded. I made sure to emphasize that this program had been a turning point for me, not only teaching me the nuts and bolts of personal finance but also giving me the confidence to face challenges head-on.

I ended with, "The biggest thing I learned is that anyone, regardless of where you start or what mistakes you've made, can turn things around. Two years ago I was afraid to check my bank balance; now I check it with a sense of accomplishment. I'm not wealthy or anything, hey, I'm a public university employee," I joked, earning some chuckles. "But I feel in control and optimistic. And you all will too. Trust the process, lean on each other, and celebrate every little win."

Just as I finished speaking, the meeting room door swung open and in hurried Ray, still in his work boots and slightly out of breath. A fine layer of drywall dust on his sleeves hinted that he'd come straight from a job site. He gave an apologetic little wave. "Sorry I'm late," he whispered as he found an empty chair Jim had saved for him at the front.

Jim flashed a grin. "Perfect timing! Everyone, this is Ray, another member of our first cohort. I'm so glad he made it. Ray, would you like to share a bit about where you are now?"

Ray nodded and stood up, scanning the room with a warm smile. He introduced himself and explained that he used to work long hours as a construction worker, barely seeing his kids, and struggling to save anything. "I used to think buying a home was something other people did," he said. After the workshop, though, he got serious about turning that dream into reality. Ray talked about checking his credit report for the first time in ages, then steadily paying off an old medical bill and a lingering high-interest loan that had been dragging down his score. He and his wife set up automatic transfers to a savings account, even if it was just fifty bucks a month at first, and watched it grow.

"Well," Ray continued, breaking into a grin, "we finally did it. Eight months after our group graduated, my wife and I closed on our own little three-bedroom house." A few people broke into applause. He added that it wasn't easy: they stuck to a strict budget, and he picked up extra side gigs on weekends, but the sacrifice paid off. The best part? The property had a small garage apartment out back. "I fixed it up myself and now we rent it out, 'house hacking,' they call it," he said proudly. "That brings in about $750 a month and goes straight toward our mortgage." There were audible gasps and nods across the circle. Ray beamed. "If a regular guy like me can get his finances together and buy a house, trust me, y'all can too."

As the newcomers finished clapping for Ray, Jim stepped forward again, eyes twinkling. "And we have one more treat tonight," he announced. "I'd like you to meet Darren." He gestured toward the back. I watched as Darren stood up and made his way to the front, hands clasped loosely behind his back. Though he was dressed casually in jeans and a t-shirt, he had the unmistakable straight-backed posture of someone used to standing at attention.

"Evening, everyone," Darren began, his voice calm and confident. "I'm Darren and I'm a workshop facilitator in training." He winked in Jim's direction. "My objective is to bring Jim's teachings on personal finance to military bases worldwide, educating our service men and women on how best to manage their money. This is desperately needed in military circles."

"I was part of this workshop's first cohort, just like these folks." He gave a modest nod in our direction. "But I kind of disappeared for a while because, well, duty called, I was deployed overseas with the Army most of this past year." A few people murmured wow, and the young man in the work uniform sat up a little straighter. Darren offered a slight smile. "I'm not really supposed to talk details about where I was," he joked lightly, "or else I'd have to kill ya." The room chuckled, and the ice was broken. "What I can tell you," he continued, "is that even out there in the desert, I was putting into practice everything we learned about managing money."

Darren explained how he set up automatic allotments from his military pay, so that roughly 20% went straight into savings and his Thrift Savings Plan (the military's 401(k)) every month. "I figured, I'm out there with food and housing provided and nowhere to spend money, might as well save it," he said. "By the time I got home, I had a solid emergency fund and then some." Some of the attendees looked amazed.

He then got a bit more serious, his brow furrowing. He told them about the pitfalls he'd seen: fellow soldiers getting trapped by payday loans with sky-high interest, or buddies back home texting him about some 'surefire' cryptocurrency scheme they'd heard about online. "Scammers are everywhere," Darren warned, "especially online. There are these so-called money gurus on YouTube and Instagram promising to make you rich overnight, or telling you to put all your cash into the next hot thing." He paused, making eye contact with a few of the attendees. "Trust me, if someone promises you can double your money in a week, it's too good to be true. I work in military intelligence, I've seen some of these schemes up close, and they are not what they seem."

The room was completely silent except for Darren's steady voice. "The best thing you can do is stick to the basics: budget, save, invest slow and steady. It's not flashy, but it works. And always do your homework if you're investing in something new. If I can keep saving money and staying cautious even while I'm thousands of miles away, you all can do it here at home." When he finished, the silence hung for a beat, and then the room erupted in appreciative applause for his candid, no-nonsense advice.

As the last of us finished speaking, I saw glimmers of hope in the attendees' eyes, the kind that comes when you realize the light at the end of the tunnel might not be a train after all.

After the workshop ended, the attendees swarmed us with questions, and we stayed late to chat. Sofia gave the young teacher in the group her number, promising to help her set up a spreadsheet like the one she'd used to pay off her debt. Dante exchanged emails with an older gentleman who wanted to break into the tech industry. Ray was immediately approached by a couple of the guys who wanted to know more about fixing credit and buying a home; he eagerly scribbled down the name of the first-time homebuyer program he used and told them to call him anytime. At the same time, Darren had a small circle gathered around him as he shared a few extra pointers on spotting scams, one older woman confessed she had nearly signed up for an expensive "financial guru" webinar, and Darren smiled and told her she'd done the right thing by trusting her gut. I found myself deep in conversation with the single mom, reassuring her that Lisa (who unfortunately couldn't make it tonight because she had an evening class, but sent her regards) had been exactly where she is now, and that today Lisa was on track to a much brighter future.

That single mom said quietly, "Hearing you all... it's the first time I feel like maybe I won't always be struggling. Thank you." I felt tears prick my eyes as I squeezed her hand. "You got this," I told her warmly.

Finally, as the library was closing up, I stepped outside, the warm night air wrapping around us. Our group, what we lovingly now call our "money family" (with Darren back in the fold), lingered on the sidewalk under the streetlights, catching up and basking in the afterglow of the evening.

Darren was with us, and after months of only sporadic contact, we peppered him with questions about how he was doing. He chuckled and said, "I'm just glad to be home," but we all knew how much more was behind those words. He couldn't tell us much about his deployment (of course), but hearing his voice and laughter again made our circle feel whole.

Ray was there too, still in his dusty work clothes, positively glowing from the night's events. "Guess what?" he asked us all, with a glint in his eye. " I quit my job and went off on my own, starting *Ray's Construction Services LLC*, my very own company! For the past two weeks my crew and I have been working on our first home remodel job." He was absolutely glowing as if he had been waiting all this time to share this news with us in person. "What's really cool is that I pay myself the same rate I earned with my former employer, but as the owner I also get to keep the company profits. Of course I also carry all the risk, but I know the industry and trade well, so think I can handle it. I'll tell you more about it…"

Lisa arrived straight from work, her scrubs peeking out from under a sweater, looking tired but radiant. Since she graduated as a dental hygienist 6 months ago she had been thriving.

Higher income and more time with Marisol since no more night classes. "For the first time," she said, voice quavering with emotion as we all crowded around, "I can afford to not only cover all our bills comfortably, but also save for Marisol's college each month." We all hugged her tight as she laughed and wiped away happy tears. The joy in that moment was infectious.

Our celebration moved to a nearby ice cream shop, an Austin favorite known for unique flavors. We indulged in scoops of lavender honey and Mexican vanilla and, for once, none of us even thought to feel guilty about spending the $5. We'd budgeted for this, after all, celebrating wins was part of the plan.

As we sat out on the patio in the warm night, eating our ice cream, I marveled at the scene. At the start of this journey, I'd felt utterly alone with my money fears. Now I was surrounded by friends who were more like family, each of us achieving goals one step at a time:

Ray, between spoonfuls of mint chocolate chip, excitedly continuing his journey to launch his own construction business. He admitted it was scary leaving the security of a steady paycheck, and he's still learning the ropes of being a contractor, like setting aside money for taxes and paying for his own health insurance now, but he was beaming with pride. He shared how a mentor from a nonprofit program called SCORE had helped him write a business plan and figure out the startup costs. He had started the process of setting up a formal entity some months ago, then developed his marketing and outreach campaigns to find customers. We all clinked our ice cream cups to toast his first customer and first job. He said that once his company finds its footing, he dreams of volunteering as a SCORE mentor himself, to help other newbies in business.

Ray was also still gushing about having his own home, brainstorming with Sofia about starting a veggie garden in his yard come spring (partly to save on groceries, mostly because it's been his dream), and bragging that his little rental unit was making a huge difference in offsetting his mortgage. His grin was so wide it almost made my cheeks hurt just looking at him. Ray was a busy guy on the move!

Lisa told us how Marisol, now a spunky ten-year-old, had proudly announced to her class that her mom "fixes people's teeth." And apparently Marisol has decided she wants to go to UT someday to become a teacher, which prompted Sofia to throw an arm around Lisa and promise to tutor Marisol in math anytime.

Dante had just finished his first year in the MBA program and admitted it was tougher than he expected balancing classes with full-time work. Still, he was proud to share that he'd landed a promotion at his company into a project management role, something he credited partly to the leadership skills he was honing in school. He grinned and said the late nights were paying off, literally, since the raise helped him keep chipping away at his tuition bills without taking on extra loans.

Kevin had dialed in on a video call from Seattle just to be part of our celebration, his face was on Dante's phone screen, propped up against the napkin holder. He was thriving in his new city, having already gotten a promotion at his tech firm.

True to form, he proudly announced that his net worth had just turned positive because he'd finally finished paying off the last of his student loans with a chunk of his most recent performance bonus. We cheered as if he'd won the lottery, and he laughed, telling us that in a way, it felt like he had.

Sofia laughing as she recounted how she introduced a mini personal finance project in her English classes. She had her students interview someone about a money lesson and write a short story about it, sneaking in a bit of financial education alongside the literature. "Who says you can't learn about compound interest in English class?" she joked. She was determined to give her students a head start we never had, and her enthusiasm was contagious.

Darren, normally so reserved, grinning as he told a funny anecdote about how his buddies overseas started calling him "Captain 20%" after he convinced a few of them to automatically save part of their pay. He said being back home made him realize he wanted to do more to help people avoid the scams and traps he'd warned us about. He mused about possibly volunteering through his church or a community center to teach a basic money safety class. We all gave him a hearty pat on the back, telling him that a lot of folks could benefit from his experience and no-BS advice.

Kayla showed up midway through dessert, sliding into an empty chair with a wide grin. She raised her spoon like a toast. "Big news," she said, her eyes shining. "Over the past year, I saved every single dollar from my freelance projects. One hundred percent. Tonight, I made the last payment on my medical debt. I'm finally free of it." We erupted in cheers. She laughed, adding, "It was brutal sometimes, two jobs, eighty-hour weeks, more late nights than I care to remember, but worth it. Debt-free tastes even better than this ice cream."

Later, while listening in on Dante and Kevin's call, she teased them about their ongoing stock debate. "Tell you what," she said, practically glowing. "Maybe I should build your company a mobile app to track the market better. I'll give you a good discount, my friend." Dante cracked up, shaking his head, and the whole table joined in the laughter.

And me, Maya, soaking it all in, feeling content and, yes, truly prosperous. Not prosperous in the millionaire sense, but in the sense that I had what I needed, plus the knowledge and stability to keep building toward what I wanted, and the ability to help others do the same.

I remembered something Jim said in that very first session: that financial literacy can change lives. Looking around at my friends, I knew he was right. It had changed each of our lives in profound ways. But it wasn't just the knowledge itself; it was the empowerment that came with it, and the friendships formed through sharing our struggles.

As the night deepened and our group finally began to part ways, with hugs all around and promises about our next get-together (a budget-friendly camping trip at a state park that Sofia was organizing, much to this city girl's apprehension), I walked to my car with Dante and Sofia.

Before we each headed home, we paused for a moment to take in the Austin skyline glowing in the distance. The UT Tower's light shone warmly, and beyond it the city twinkled with life. This city had challenged us with its high cost of living and rapid pace, but it had also given us the opportunities that brought us together.

"You know," Dante mused, breaking the silence as we gazed at the skyline, "we should write a book or something. *Financial Freedom Fighters of Austin,*" he quipped, striking a superhero pose.

Sofia lit up. "Yes! Or at least a social media channel," she said, turning to us eagerly. "We have so many tips now, so many stories. Think of how many people out there are like we were, feeling hopeless and alone. We could totally do something to reach them." Her eyes were practically sparkling with ideas. "Dante, I've always thought of you like a big brother, especially with finance stuff. You'd be great sharing your experiences and advice with others as you've done with me!"

As we stood there laughing about possible channel names, Dante's phone buzzed. It was a text from Kevin up in Seattle, who had still been listening on speakerphone until a moment ago. He'd caught the tail end of our conversation. *Count me in!* the text read. *I've started helping with a financial literacy club at the university here. People really need this info. If you guys launch a social media channel, I'll be your first subscriber!* I smiled, heart warm with pride at how even far away, Kevin was paying it forward too.

I chuckled and put my arm around Sofia. "Maybe someday," I said. "For now, I'm just happy mentoring others through Jim's workshops, or even at the library when I can. Remember that budget class I ran here last month? It felt great to help people get a handle on things. I'm good just living by example for now."

We stood there a moment longer, each of us lost in thought. I silently thanked my past self for having the courage to click that RSVP to the free workshop 2+ years ago. What a journey it sparked.

Finally, we said our goodnights. I climbed into my trusty old Honda (still chugging along at 15 years old, and though I've saved enough to replace it when it decides to retire, I really do enjoy NOT having a car payment). Driving home with the windows down to catch the cool hint of fall in the breeze, I found myself reflecting on the meaning of prosperity. It used to be such a distant word to me, conjuring images of mansions or fancy cars or some life that ordinary people don't live. Now I understand it differently. Prosperity is having enough, and then some, enough to meet your needs, some extra to enjoy life, and some to share with others. By that definition, we were all truly prosperous, or at least well on our way.

At a red light, I caught sight of the marquee of a theater by the road: "Keep Austin Thriving" it read, a playful twist on the city's famous slogan "Keep Austin Weird." I smiled to myself. Thriving, yes, that's what we were doing.

When I got home, I found a letter from my mom waiting in the mailbox. Inside was a belated birthday card (she never forgets; I'd turned 29 a couple of weeks ago) and a handwritten note:

I'm so proud of you, Maya.
I brag to my friends
about how smart you are
with your money now!
- Love, Mom

I pressed the note to my chest, tears of joy welling up. Mom had struggled her whole life with money, and for years I'd wished I could do more for her. Now I finally felt equipped to help as my own stability grew. In fact, I had already started sending her a little extra cash each month to make things easier, and I'd been quietly building a "Mom fund" to surprise her with a trip to Austin for a real vacation, she'd never seen much beyond her neighborhood in San Antonio.

I looked around my cozy apartment. It wasn't fancy, mostly secondhand furniture, a tiny kitchen, an AC unit that rattled, but it was home and it was within my means. In that moment, it felt like a palace because of the security and peace of mind I now had.

There was a time when I thought money was nothing but a source of anxiety and shame. Now I see it as a tool, one I'm finally learning to master. And like any tool, its true value comes from what you build with it. We weren't just building better bank balances; we were building better lives, for ourselves, our families, and even our community as we started to spread the knowledge.

Before getting ready for bed, I took one last peek at my budget spreadsheet on my laptop (old habits die hard, and I actually enjoy updating it now). I entered the $5 ice cream expense with a grin, probably the happiest five bucks I've ever spent. I scrolled through the categories on my screen, there were new ones now like "Vacation Fund" and "Investments," in place of old ones like "Overdraft Fees" and "Credit Card Minimums." It was tangible proof of how far I'd come.

Of course, I also had to check on my net worth. Some big changes over the past year, new job, new approach to personal finances.

Net Worth = Assets - Liabilities			
Assets		**Liabilities**	
401(k)	$12,972	Credit Cards	$0
Investments	$4,467	Student Debt	$16,750
Savings	$10,400		
Total	$27,839	Total	$16,750
Net Worth =		**$11,089**	

Just 6 months ago my net worth hit zero, a big accomplishment after year of being negative. Another 6 months and I'm POSITIVE $11,089. Still in my 20's and better than average… and I'm just getting started!

I was already visualizing my future targets in 5 years. Based on my current earnings and newfound approach to saving and investing I know I can do great things financially. I opened my notebook app and jotted down where I want to be in 5 years:

<u>My 5 Year Money Goals</u>

401(k) - $60k

Investments - $20k

Savings - $35k

Student Debt – PAID OFF!

Buy New (Used) Car

Buy a HOUSE!

And.... Net Worth of $100k+++

My story had improved dramatically, through hard work and smart planning. I could write my own ticket, financially and otherwise. And the best part? I wasn't doing it alone. We were all out there writing our success stories together and helping others start theirs.

Closing the laptop, I whispered a "thank you", to Jim for teaching us, to my friends for sharing this journey, and to myself for sticking with it even when it was hard.

My phone dinged so I must have forgotten to switch to silent mode for the night. It was a group text from Dante: "*Guys, I just set up a YouTube channel, called Big Bro Finance, and posted my first short video about saving 20% - thanks Darren for that inspiration. Send me your stories and I'll post. Follow me @bigbrofin on YouTube, TikTok, and Instagram!*"

So cool. I know he'll be able to reach a lot of people with his supportive, calm, and measured approach to teaching personal finance. You go Dante!

As I turned out the light, I felt a wave of contentment and optimism that would have astonished the me of a year ago. Tomorrow was payday, and for once I wasn't counting down the hours in dread or desperation. In fact, I was looking forward to it, excited to automatically invest a chunk of it, pay myself first, and maybe even set a little aside for that next trip or class I'd been daydreaming about.

Lying in the dark, the distant hum of the city lulling me to sleep, I realized that in helping each other find financial freedom, we'd gained something even more valuable: the freedom to dream again. And *that* is prosperity, indeed.

Appendix: Key Concepts

Throughout the story, Jim guided the group through practical lessons on money, lessons designed to build a foundation for prosperity. What follows is a summary of the key concepts he covered. Think of this section as a quick reference guide you can return to anytime you need a refresher.

1. Earning Money

Income can come from many sources, traditional W-2 jobs, side hustles, freelance work (1099 income), entrepreneurship, or military service. What matters most is understanding the difference between gross pay (what you earn before taxes and deductions) and net, or *take-home*, pay (what actually lands in your account). The sooner you recognize how money flows in, the easier it becomes to plan how it flows out.

2. Saving

Savings provide both stability and freedom. Jim described three types:

- **Emergency savings**: 3–6 months of essentials like rent, food, and utilities. SAVE THIS FIRST!
- **Planned savings**: for irregular but certain costs, such as car repairs or annual insurance.
- **Targeted savings**: for specific goals, from a new laptop to a first home.

A good practice is to save consistently, aiming for at least 20% of your take-home income. Savings are what keep you from being forced into debt when life throws you a curveball.

3. Spending

Spending wisely is about priorities, not deprivation. A simple guideline is the **50-30-20 rule**: 50% of income toward needs, 30% toward wants, and 20% toward savings or debt repayment. Save the 20% FIRST, and then pay for needs and wants with what's left.

Budgeting is the tool that makes this balance possible. Avoiding impulse purchases, "buy now, pay later" schemes, and high-interest traps preserves financial freedom. And always remember, inflation slowly erodes the value of money, which makes disciplined spending even more important.

4. Debt & Credit

Debt can either help you build a future or trap you in the past. **Good debt**, such as a mortgage or reasonable student loans, can support long-term goals. **Bad debt**, like carrying a balance on high-interest credit cards, drains wealth. Credit is powerful, but it must be handled wisely: pay on time, keep balances low, and avoid opening too many accounts. A strong credit score can determine whether you qualify for a loan, secure an apartment, or even land a job. Co-signing loans is risky, and defaulting can damage your financial life for years.

5. Big Buys: Cars and Homes

Cars lose value the moment you drive them off the lot, which makes buying used and avoiding costly add-ons the smartest choice. Leasing often looks appealing but usually costs more over time. Homes, by contrast, often grow in value but come with ongoing costs: mortgages, taxes, insurance, and upkeep. Understanding concepts like DTI (Debt-to-Income ratio), PMI (Private Mortgage Insurance), and federal loan programs

(FHA, VA, USDA) is essential. Renting may make sense in the short term, while ownership builds equity in the long term.

6. Investing

Investing is how money grows. Whether through stocks, bonds, mutual funds, or ETFs, the principle is the same: risk and reward go hand in hand. The earlier you start, the more you benefit from **compound interest**, where your money earns not only on the original amount but also on past earnings. Diversification - spreading investments across different assets, lowers risk. Above all, investing is a long-term strategy, not gambling.

7. Education & Career Choices

Education is one of the most important financial decisions you'll ever make. Trade schools, community colleges, four-year universities, and entrepreneurship all come with different costs and potential returns. Scholarships and grants reduce the need for loans, and every choice should be evaluated for its return on investment. The goal is not just a degree but a career path that supports your financial and personal goals.

8. Net Worth & Financial Independence

Income is important, but wealth is best measured by **net worth**: assets minus liabilities. Assets include savings, investments, and property. Liabilities are debts and obligations. Growing assets while reducing liabilities steadily builds financial health. The ultimate destination is financial independence, the freedom to choose how you live and work because money no longer dictates your options.

9. Avoiding Financial Pitfalls

Financial progress can be undone quickly by poor decisions or unexpected setbacks. Scams and predatory lenders prey on desperation, while lifestyle inflation (spending more as you earn more) quietly erodes savings. Insurance is an essential safeguard, protecting against the emergencies — medical, auto, or home-related — that could otherwise cause financial disaster.

10. Giving Back & Prosperity

Jim closed his sessions with an important reminder: prosperity is about more than money. True wealth includes purpose, impact, and community. Sharing what you've learned, helping others, and giving back creates a ripple effect that strengthens not just your own future but also the world around you.

About the Author

David G. Gatchell is a proud father of two wonderful children, financial literacy educator, author, and creator of tools that help people break free from economic struggle. He is the author of *The Financial Empowerment Handbook*, the foundational text for his financial literacy programs taught to schools and diverse community groups across the country.

David is the founder of Four Gifts Publishing, a platform dedicated to developing relatable, high-impact financial education materials. He also created the Finance IQ Test, a first-of-its-kind diagnostic tool that measures financial knowledge and decision-making in real-world scenarios.

As the Founder and Executive Director of nonprofit Prospera Literacy, David leads community-focused initiatives that promote both financial and technical fluency, two pillars he believes are essential to prosperity in the modern world.

Motivated by his own early struggles and driven by a deep desire to level the playing field, David's mission is simple: make prosperity possible for everyone, especially those who've been left out of the conversation for far too long.

A Note from the Publisher

Thank you for reading *Steps to Prosperity*. We hope this story gave you not only something to think about, but something to act on.

At Four Gifts Publishing, our mission is to help more people build lives of financial confidence and freedom. That's why we've created a tool to help you take the next step.

How much do you really know about money? The Finance IQ Test is a 30-minute, 50-question assessment designed to help you gauge your knowledge across key areas of personal finance, including earning, saving, spending, debt, credit, investing, and more.

Whether you're just getting started or already on your journey to financial empowerment, this test will help you:

- Identify what you already know
- And discover areas where you can grow

Take the Finance IQ Test: scan the QR code below or visit: www.financeIQtest.com

We created this tool for people just like you, curious, capable, and ready to take control of their financial future. Let's build something better, starting with what we know, and growing from there.

The Team at Four Gifts Publishing

www.ingramcontent.com/pod-product-compliance
Lightning Source LLC
LaVergne TN
LVHW100315210926
848480LV00003B/1133
* 9 7 9 8 9 8 6 7 2 0 0 6 7 *